Guide to
NORTHEAST PACIFIC
Flatfishes

Families Bothidae, Cynoglossidae, and Pleuronectidae

Donald E. Kramer • William H. Barss
Brian C. Paust • Barry E. Bracken

Illustrated by Terry Josey

Sea Grant

Alaska Sea Grant College Program
University of Alaska Fairbanks
P.O. Box 755040
Fairbanks, Alaska 99775-5040
(907) 474-6707 • Fax (907) 474-6285

AFDF

Alaska Fisheries Development Foundation
508 West Second Avenue, Suite 212
Anchorage, Alaska 99501-2208

Marine Advisory Bulletin No. 47 • 1995 • $20.00

Elmer E. Rasmuson Library Cataloging-in-Publication Data

Guide to northeast Pacific flatfishes : families Bothidae, Cynoglossidae, and
  Pleuronectidae / by Donald E. Kramer ... [et al.]

  (Marine advisory bulletin ; no. 47)

    1. Flatfishes—Identification.   2. Flatfishes—North Pacific Ocean.
3. Bothidae.   4. Cynoglossidae.   5. Pleuronectidae.   I. Kramer, Donald E.
II. Alaska Sea Grant College Program.   III. Alaska Fisheries Development
Foundation.   IV. Series.

QL637.9.P5G85 1995

ISBN 1-56612-032-2

Credits

This book is the result of work sponsored by the University of Alaska Sea
Grant College Program, which is cooperatively supported by the U.S. Department of Commerce, NOAA Office of Sea Grant and Extramural Programs,
under grant no. NA46RG0104, projects A/71-01 and A/75-01; and by the
University of Alaska with state funds. The University of Alaska is an affirma-
tive action/equal opportunity employer and educational institution.

    Sea Grant is a unique partnership with public and private sectors com-
bining research, education, and technology transfer for public service. This
national network of universities meets changing environmental and eco-
nomic needs of people in our coastal, ocean, and Great Lakes regions.

Contents

Family Pleuronectidae (continued)

Preface

The primary purpose of this guide is to simplify the identification of flatfish found along the Pacific coast of North America. It is intended for those who do not have the experience or the time to use a scientific key for identification. The guide is useful for commercial fishermen, fish processors, and fisheries managers. Recreational fishermen can use the photographs and illustrations to identify the species they see. Divers who don't collect fish for later identification will also find the book helpful. The book is printed on water resistant paper to withstand hard wear and wet conditions.

While the guide is primarily for identification of flatfish species in Alaska waters, it includes all species along the Pacific coast of North America south to the California Baja California border. Thirty of the thirty-nine species in this book have been reported in Alaska waters—by adding nine species the authors have extended the guide's utility over a much larger area.

Species are arranged in the book by family rather than by color or other physical character, and families are arranged alphabetically: Bothidae, Cynoglossidae, and Pleuronectidae. Users of the guide can page through the book and select all possibilities for the specimen to be identified, then determine the correct name by using the distinguishing characters in the illustrations and photos. As an aid to narrowing the possibilities, species lists based on anal spine, lateral line shape, and length of the accessory dorsal branch are presented on pages 7–9.

This guide does not include a key to flatfishes. Keys can be found in *Pacific Fishes of Canada,* by J.S. Hart; *Annotated Key to the Fishes of Alaska,* by R. Baxter; and *Guide to the Coastal Marine Fishes of California,* by D.J. Miller and R.N. Lea.

We hope this guide is of practical use to the fishing industry. We also hope recreational fishermen and divers can find greater enjoyment in their sport by being able to identify the flatfish they see or catch.

Donald E. Kramer
William H. Barss
Brian C. Paust
Barry E. Bracken

About the Authors

Don Kramer is professor of seafood technology at the University of Alaska Fairbanks School of Fisheries and Ocean Sciences. He is chairman and seafood specialist for the Alaska Sea Grant Marine Advisory Program, where he has worked since 1980. Kramer also was research scientist with the Canadian Department of Fisheries and Oceans for 14 years. His research interests are the handling, processing, and storage of fish and shellfish.

Bill Barss has been a marine fish and wildlife biologist with the Oregon Department of Fish and Wildlife since 1971, working with groundfish management and research. In recent years his duties have involved underwater research with submersibles and the Pacific whiting fishery. His many publications on groundfish include a booklet on rockfish identification. He is currently the coordinator for the Pacific whiting shoreside observation program.

Brian Paust has worked with the Alaska Sea Grant Program in several capacities since 1978. He has conducted a variety of practical commercial fisheries research projects and has published materials ranging from octopus fisheries to business strategies used in the development of coldwater bivalve aquaculture. Paust is associate professor at the University of Alaska Fairbanks and marine advisory agent in Petersburg, Alaska.

Barry Bracken has held a number of positions with the Alaska Department of Fish and Game since 1967 and has been the Region 1 Groundfish Project leader since 1978. In his current position, he has research and management responsibility for state-managed groundfish in the eastern Gulf of Alaska. Bracken is a member of the North Pacific Fishery Management Council's Gulf of Alaska Groundfish Team and the Canada/U.S. Groundfish Technical Subcommittee.

Donald E. Kramer
Marine Advisory Program
School of Fisheries and
    Ocean Sciences
University of Alaska Fairbanks
2221 E. Northern Lights Blvd.
Anchorage, Alaska 99508-4140

Brian C. Paust
Marine Advisory Program
School of Fisheries and
    Ocean Sciences
University of Alaska Fairbanks
P.O. Box 1329
Petersburg, Alaska 99833

William H. Barss
Marine Region, Finfish Program
Oregon Dept. of Fish and Wildlife
2040 SE Marine Science Ctr. Dr.
Newport, Oregon 97365-5294

Barry E. Bracken
Division of Commercial Fisheries
Management and Development
Alaska Dept. of Fish and Game
P.O. Box 667
Petersburg, Alaska 99833

Acknowledgments

The authors wish to thank Jeff Fargo and Tyson Vogeler, who reviewed the manuscript. We also thank M. James Allen, Kunio Amaoka, and Doyne W. Kessler for reviewing species descriptions.

Flatfish photographs were taken by the authors and the following: Kunio Amaoka, Ann Dalkey, Darrin Greenstein, Peter L. Haaker, Doyne W. Kessler, Milton S. Love, Douglas F. Markle, James Meehan, Wayne A. Palsson, Nevill L. Venables, and the Oregon Department of Fish and Wildlife. We are grateful to M. James Allen, Marvin Epps, Schon Hardy, Richard MacIntosh, Tyson Vogeler, David Watson, the Monterey Bay Public Aquarium, and the University of Alaska Anchorage Fishery Observer Training Center for providing flatfish specimens to be photographed.

Illustrations were done by Terry Josey. Editing is by Laurie McNicholas and Sue Keller; layout and format is by Carol Kaynor, Susan Gibson, Kalei Kagawa, and Judy Hargis; cover design is by Kurt Byers and Susan Gibson; and cover art (of starry flounder) is by Susan Ogle.

The Alaska Fisheries Development Foundation provided funds for the illustrations, and the Alaska Sea Grant College Program provided pre-publication and funds for printing. Support for the authors was furnished by the Alaska Sea Grant College Program, the Alaska Department of Fish and Game, and the Oregon Department of Fish and Wildlife.

Special thanks go to Ron Dearborn, director of the Alaska Sea Grant College Program; and Mel Monsen, former executive director of the Alaska Fisheries Development Foundation, for encouragement to complete this guide.

Introduction

Flatfishes are unique in that the skull is asymmetrical with both eyes on the same side of the head. Flatfish begin life like symmetrical fish, with an eye on each side of the head. A few days after hatching, one eye begins to migrate and soon both eyes are close together on one side. Flatfish spend the rest of their lives on or near the bottom with the eyed side facing up. The blind side is usually a paler color (most often white or off-white) than the eyed side. If the right eye migrates to the left side, the flatfish is left-eyed (sinistral). If the left eye migrates to the right side, the fish is right-eyed (dextral).

Flatfish are in the order Pleuronectiformes (sometimes called Heterosomata). Worldwide there are more than 500 species of flatfishes, in six or seven families. Flatfishes include flounders, soles, turbots, halibuts, sanddabs, plaices, and tonguefishes. These names do not indicate that a fish belongs to a specific family; for example, species referred to as sole occur in Bothidae, Pleuronectidae, and Soleidae. Flatfishes found in North American waters are in two broad categories—one includes the families Bothidae and Pleuronectidae, and the other includes the families Cynoglossidae and Soleidae.

The Bothidae is a very large family with more than 200 species, seven of which are found along the Pacific coast of North America. The family is called the left-eyed flounders because the eyes and dark color typically are on the left side. However, in two of the seven Pacific coast species (California halibut and fantail sole), the eyes can be on the left side or the right side. The Bothidae are closely related to the Pleuronectidae.

The Cynoglossidae is made up of about 100 species of tonguefishes. Their eyes are on the left side and the dorsal and anal fins are joined to the pointed caudal fin. Only one species in the family occurs along the Pacific coast of North America, the California tonguefish. Cynoglossidae species are closely related to Soleidae; in fact the American Fisheries Society lists all members of the two families in Soleidae. Soleidae also includes species with the eyes on the right side and a distinct caudal fin that is not pointed.

The Pleuronectidae is composed of right-eyed flounders, with the eyes and dark color usually on the right side. This family includes about 100 species, 31 of which are found along the Pacific coast of North America. Only one of the 31 species (the starry flounder) regularly has the eyes on either the left or right side of the head. The Pacific halibut occasionally breaks the rule and is left-eyed.

Using This Guide to Identify Flatfish

The purpose of this guide is to provide enough information to easily identify flatfish, without using a scientific key. The photographs and illustrations showing the important features of each species can be used to identify a fish. The labeled illustrations of flatfish on pages 3–6 serve as a basis for interpreting species descriptons and illustrations throughout the book. They show external characters, how flatfish are measured, pelvic fin symmetry, caudal fin shape, and mouth position.

Three features that are easy to check can be used to narrow the range of possibilities for an unknown fish. These features are the anal spine, shape of the lateral line, and presence or absence of an accessory dorsal branch.

The anal spine is located at the front of the anal fin. It points toward the head of the fish, and may be strong or weak and exposed or embedded. Locate the anal spine by running a finger back along the abdominal ridge from the pelvic fins to the anal fin. It may be necessary to use a fingernail to find a spine that is small and embedded.

The lateral line above the pectoral fin can be straight, curved, or arched. The characteristic shape of the lateral line for each species can be seen on both the eyed and blind sides.

The accessory dorsal branch is a branch of the lateral line. It starts near the head and runs back just below the dorsal fin. It may be easier to find on the blind side, but it is sometimes shorter there so both sides should be examined.

Throughout the book, the lengths given for fish are fork lengths. Depths are in fathoms (fm); 1 fathom = 6 feet.

> To identify a flatfish, look for the anal spine, lateral line, and an accessory dorsal branch and use the species lists on pages 7, 8, and 9 to make a list of possible names. Then compare the fish being identified with illustrations and photographs of each species on your list, using pages 3–6 as a guide. This task will be further simplified if you know where the fish was taken, because you can use range information to eliminate some of the possible species.

External Characters of Flatfish

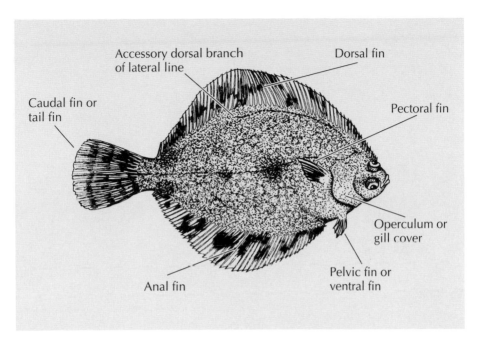

Accessory dorsal branch of lateral line

Dorsal fin

Caudal fin or tail fin

Pectoral fin

Operculum or gill cover

Anal fin

Pelvic fin or ventral fin

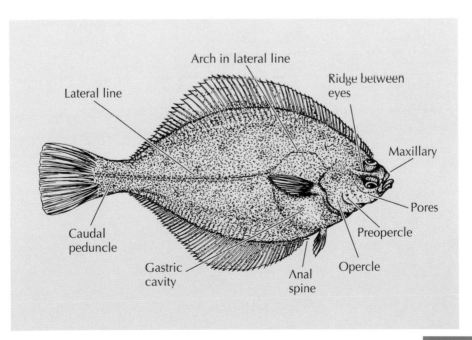

Arch in lateral line

Ridge between eyes

Lateral line

Maxillary

Pores

Caudal peduncle

Preopercle

Gastric cavity

Anal spine

Opercle

Flatfish Measurements

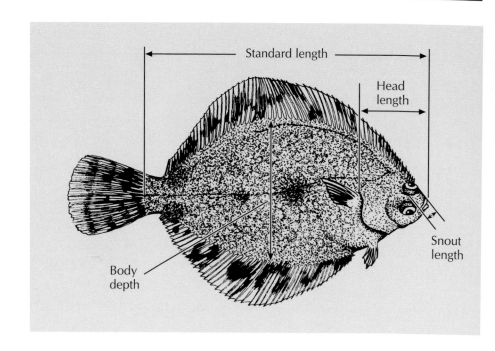

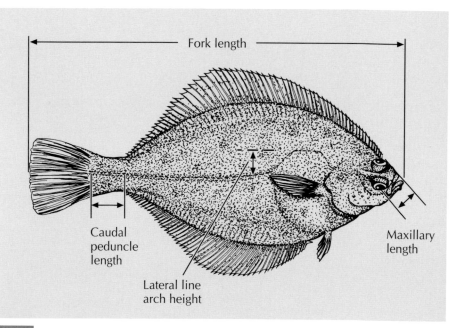

Caudal Fin Shapes

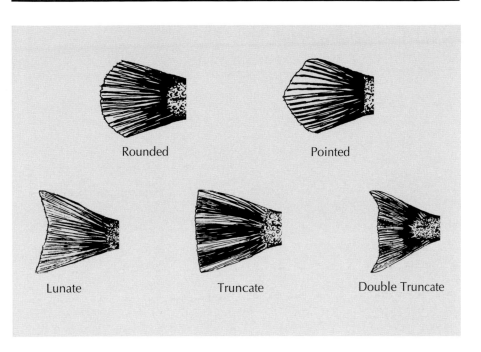

Rounded

Pointed

Lunate

Truncate

Double Truncate

Mouth Measurements

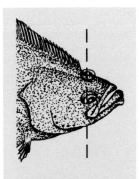

Maxillary extends to below posterior edge of eye socket; sometimes goes past posterior edge of eye socket.

Maxillary extends to below eye socket.

Maxillary extends to anterior edge of eye socket; sometimes does not reach anterior edge of eye socket.

Pelvic Fin Symmetry

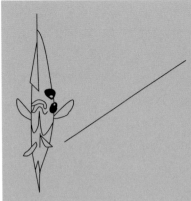

Pelvic fins asymmetrically placed.
Eyed-side fin inserts on abdominal ridge.
Blind-side fin inserts off abdominal ridge.

Family Bothidae

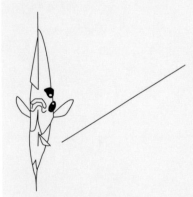

One pelvic fin located on eyed side.
No pelvic fin on blind side.

Family Cynoglossidae

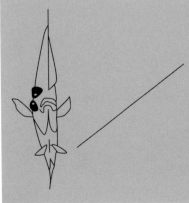

Pelvic fins symmetrically placed.
Fins insert one on each side of abdominal ridge.

Family Pleuronectidae

List of Species—Anal Spine

See page 3 for anal spine illustration.

Anal Spine Absent

Gulf Sanddab (p. 12)
Citharichthys fragilis

Pacific Sanddab (p. 14)
Citharichthys sordidus

Speckled Sanddab (p. 16)
Citharichthys stigmaeus

Longfin Sanddab (p. 18)
Citharichthys xanthostigma

California Halibut (p. 22)
Paralichthys californicus

Fantail Sole (p. 26)
Xystreurys liolepis

California Tonguefish (p. 30)
Symphurus atricauda

Scalyeye Plaice (p. 32)
Acanthopsetta nadeshnyi

Kamchatka Flounder (p. 34)
Atheresthes evermanni

Arrowtooth Flounder (p. 36)
Atheresthes stomias

Roughscale Sole (p. 38)
Clidoderma asperrimum

Deepsea Sole (p. 40)
Embassichthys bathybius

Dover Sole (p. 60)
Microstomus pacificus

Greenland Halibut (p. 94)
Reinhardtius hippoglossoides

Anal Spine Present

Bigmouth Sole (p. 20)
Hippoglossina stomata

Slender Sole (p. 42)
Eopsetta exilis

Petrale Sole (p. 44)
Eopsetta jordani

Rex Sole (p. 46)
Errex zachirus

Korean Flounder (p. 48)
Glyptocephalus stelleri

Anal Spine Present *(continued)*

Flathead Sole (p. 50)
Hippoglossoides elassodon

Bering Flounder (p. 52)
Hippoglossoides robustus

Pacific Halibut (p. 54)
Hippoglossus stenolepis

Diamond Turbot (p. 56)
Hypsopsetta guttulata

Forkline Sole (p. 58)
Inopsetta ischyra

Starry Flounder (p. 62)
Platichthys stellatus

Yellowfin Sole (p. 66)
Pleuronectes asper

Rock Sole (p. 68)
Pleuronectes bilineatus

Arctic Flounder (p. 70)
Pleuronectes glacialis

Butter Sole (p. 72)
Pleuronectes isolepis

Dark Flounder (p. 74)
Pleuronectes obscurus

Longhead Dab (p. 76)
Pleuronectes proboscideus

Alaska Plaice (p. 78)
Pleuronectes quadrituberculatus

Sakhalin Sole (p. 80)
Pleuronectes sakhalinensis

English Sole (p. 82)
Pleuronectes vetulus

C-O Sole (p. 84)
Pleuronichthys coenosus

Curlfin Sole (p. 86)
Pleuronichthys decurrens

Spotted Turbot (p. 88)
Pleuronichthys ritteri

Hornyhead Turbot (p. 90)
Pleuronichthys verticalis

Sand Sole (p. 92)
Psettichthys melanostictus

List of Species—Lateral Line Shape

See pages 3–4 for lateral line illustration.

No Lateral Line
California Tonguefish (p. 30)
Symphurus atricauda

Straight to Curved Lateral Line
Gulf Sanddab (p. 12)
Citharichthys fragilis

Pacific Sanddab (p. 14)
Citharichthys sordidus

Speckled Sanddab (p. 16)
Citharichthys stigmaeus

Longfin Sanddab (p. 18)
Citharichthys xanthostigma

Kamchatka Flounder (p. 34)
Atheresthes evermanni

Arrowtooth Flounder (p. 36)
Atheresthes stomias

Slender Sole (p. 42)
Eopsetta exilis

Petrale Sole (p. 44)
Eopsetta jordani

Rex Sole (p. 46)
Errex zachirus

Korean Flounder (p. 48)
Glyptocephalus stelleri

Diamond Turbot (p. 56)
Hypsopsetta guttulata

Forkline Sole (p. 58)
Inopsetta ischyra

Dover Sole (p. 60)
Microstomus pacificus

Starry Flounder (p. 62)
Platichthys stellatus

Arctic Flounder (p. 70)
Pleuronectes glacialis

English Sole (p. 82)
Pleuronectes vetulus

C-O Sole (p. 84)
Pleuronichthys coenosus

Curlfin Sole (p. 86)
Pleuronichthys decurrens

Spotted Turbot (p. 88)
Pleuronichthys ritteri

Straight to Curved Lateral Line (continued)
Hornyhead Turbot (p. 90)
Pleuronichthys verticalis

Sand Sole (p. 92)
Psettichthys melanostictus

Greenland Halibut (p. 94)
Reinhardtius hippoglossoides

Low Arch in Lateral Line
Roughscale Sole (p. 38)
Clidoderma asperrimum

Deepsea Sole (p. 40)
Embassichthys bathybius

Flathead Sole (p. 50)
Hippoglossoides elassodon

Bering Flounder (p. 52)
Hippoglossoides robustus

Butter Sole (p. 72)
Pleuronectes isolepis

Dark Flounder (p. 74)
Pleuronectes obscurus

Medium to High Arch in Lateral Line
Bigmouth Sole (p. 20)
Hippoglossina stomata

California Halibut (p. 22)
Paralichthys californicus

Fantail Sole (p. 26)
Xystreurys liolepis

Scalyeye Plaice (p. 32)
Acanthopsetta nadeshnyi

Pacific Halibut (p. 54)
Hippoglossus stenolepis

Yellowfin Sole (p. 66)
Pleuronectes asper

Rock Sole (p. 68)
Pleuronectes bilineatus

Longhead Dab (p. 76)
Pleuronectes proboscideus

Alaska Plaice (p. 78)
Pleuronectes quadrituberculatus

Sakhalin Sole (p. 80)
Pleuronectes sakhalinensis

List of Species—Accessory Dorsal Branch

See pages 3–4 for accessory dorsal branch illustration.

No Lateral Line
California Tonguefish (p. 30)
Symphurus atricauda

No Accessory Dorsal Branch to Lateral Line (ADB)
Gulf Sanddab (p. 12)
Citharichthys fragilis

Pacific Sanddab (p. 14)
Citharichthys sordidus

Speckled Sanddab (p. 16)
Citharichthys stigmaeus

Longfin Sanddab (p. 18)
Citharichthys xanthostigma

Bigmouth Sole (p. 20)
Hippoglossina stomata

California Halibut (p. 22)
Paralichthys californicus

Fantail Sole (p. 26)
Xystreurys liolepis

Scalyeye Plaice (p. 32)
Acanthopsetta nadeshnyi

Kamchatka Flounder (p. 34)
Atheresthes evermanni

Arrowtooth Flounder (p. 36)
Atheresthes stomias

Roughscale Sole (p. 38)
Clidoderma asperrimum

Deepsea Sole (p. 40)
Embassichthys bathybius

Slender Sole (p. 42)
Eopsetta exilis

Petrale Sole (p. 44)
Eopsetta jordani

Rex Sole (p. 46)
Errex zachirus

Korean Flounder (p. 48)
Glyptocephalus stelleri

Flathead Sole (p. 50)
Hippoglossoides elassodon

Bering Flounder (p. 52)
Hippoglossoides robustus

No ADB (continued)
Pacific Halibut (p. 54)
Hippoglossus stenolepis

Dover Sole (p. 60)
Microstomus pacificus

Starry Flounder (p. 62)
Platichthys stellatus

Yellowfin Sole (p. 66)
Pleuronectes asper

Arctic Flounder (p. 70)
Pleuronectes glacialis

Dark Flounder (p. 74)
Pleuronectes obscurus

Longhead Dab (p. 76)
Pleuronectes proboscideus

Alaska Plaice (p. 78)
Pleuronectes quadrituberculatus

Sakhalin Sole (p. 80)
Pleuronectes sakhalinensis

Greenland Halibut (p. 94)
Reinhardtius hippoglossoides

Short ADB
Forkline Sole (p. 58)
Inopsetta ischyra

Rock Sole (p. 68)
Pleuronectes bilineatus

Sand Sole (p. 92)
Psettichthys melanostictus

Medium to Long ADB
Diamond Turbot (p. 56)
Hypsopsetta guttulata

Butter Sole (p. 72)
Pleuronectes isolepis

English Sole (p. 82)
Pleuronectes vetulus

C-O Sole (p. 84)
Pleuronichthys coenosus

Curlfin Sole (p. 86)
Pleuronichthys decurrens

Spotted Turbot (p. 88)
Pleuronichthys ritteri

Hornyhead Turbot (p. 90)
Pleuronichthys verticalis

North Pacific Ocean

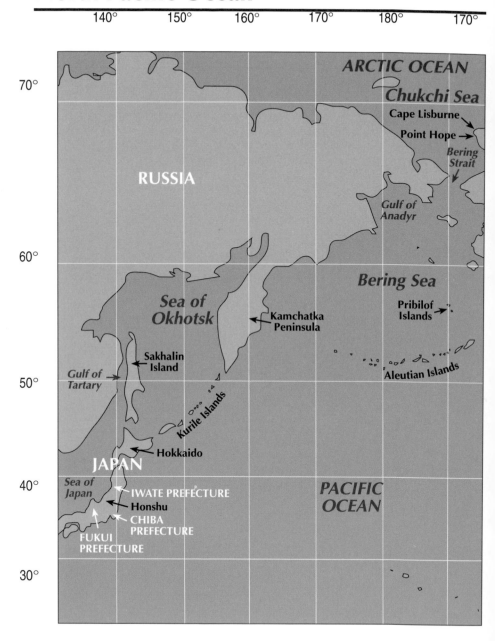

Place names on these maps are referred to in text describing flatfish distribution, pages 12–94.

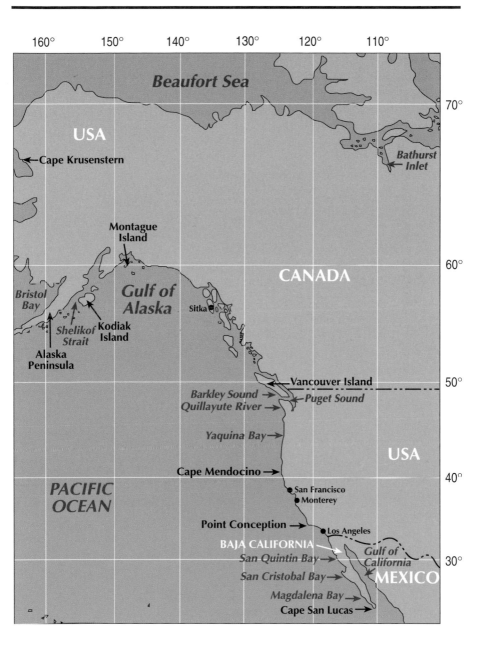

Gulf Sanddab *Citharichthys fragilis*

Description: Left-eyed. Eyed side uniform brownish color. Blind side off-white to light tan. Body elongate to oval. Caudal fin rounded. Lateral line nearly straight; accessory dorsal branch absent. Medium-sized mouth with head length 2⅔ times maxillary length. Anal spine absent. Gill rakers on lower limb of first arch are 16 to 21. Scale count in lateral line is 46 to 51.

Size: To 14 cm (6 inches).

Range and Habitat: From Manhattan Beach, southern California, south along the coast of Baja California and into the Gulf of California. Most common in the Gulf of California. From 10 to 190 fm.

Remarks: Similar to Pacific sanddab (which has smaller scales); to speckled sanddab (which has smaller scales and shorter pectoral fin); and to longfin sanddab (which has longer pectoral fin). Positive identification of gulf sanddab, Pacific sanddab, speckled sanddab, and longfin sanddab require gill raker and lateral line scale counts.

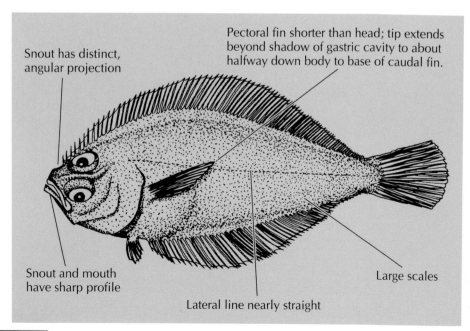

Snout has distinct, angular projection

Pectoral fin shorter than head; tip extends beyond shadow of gastric cavity to about halfway down body to base of caudal fin.

Snout and mouth have sharp profile

Large scales

Lateral line nearly straight

Gulf sanddab, eyed side.

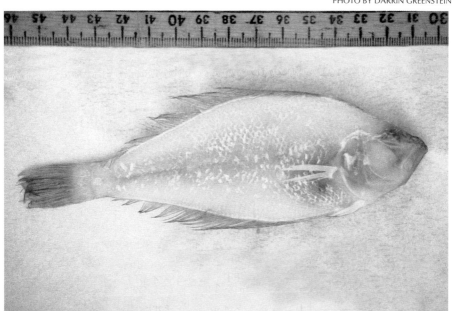

Gulf sanddab, blind side.

Pacific Sanddab
Citharichthys sordidus

(mottled sanddab, soft flounder, melgrim)

Description: Left-eyed. Eyed side dull light brown, mottled with brown or black and sometimes yellow or orange. Blind side off-white to tan. Body elongate to oval, with large scales. Caudal fin only slightly rounded. Lateral line nearly straight; accessory dorsal branch absent. Mouth medium-sized with maxillary extending below anterior part of lower eye. Eyes large. Anal spine absent. Gill rakers on lower limb of first arch are 12 to 16. Scale count in lateral line is 61 to 70.

Size: To 41 cm (16 inches). To 2 pounds, but most weigh less than ⅓ pound.

Range and Habitat: Sea of Japan, Aleutian Islands, Bering Sea, and south to Cape San Lucas, Baja California. Sand or mud-sand bottom in 5 to 300 fm; most abundant in 20 to 50 fm, rare below 100 fm. Common in shallow coastal water from British Columbia to California.

Remarks: Excellent food fish. Regarded as a delicacy in California, low commercial demand elsewhere (Oregon, Washington, British Columbia). Sometimes confused with speckled sanddab, which has black speckling on body. Positive identification of Pacific sanddab, gulf sanddab, speckled sanddab, and longfin sanddab require gill raker and lateral line scale counts.

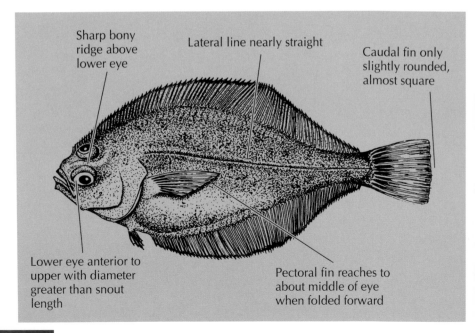

Sharp bony ridge above lower eye

Lateral line nearly straight

Caudal fin only slightly rounded, almost square

Lower eye anterior to upper with diameter greater than snout length

Pectoral fin reaches to about middle of eye when folded forward

Pacific sanddab, eyed side.

Pacific sanddab, blind side.

Speckled Sanddab *Citharichthys stigmaeus*

(Catalina sanddab)

Description: Left-eyed. Eyed side tan to olive brown, finely and sharply speckled with black. Blind side off-white to cream. Body elongate to oval. Caudal peduncle slender. Caudal fin rounded. Lateral line straight with slight slope over pectoral fin; accessory dorsal branch absent. Mouth medium-sized with maxillary extending below anterior part of eye. Eyes small to medium-sized. Anal spine absent. Gill rakers on lower limb of first arch are 8 to 10. Scale count in lateral line is 52 to 58.

Size: To 17 cm (7 inches), but rarely over 13 cm (5 inches).

Range and Habitat: Montague Island, Alaska, to Magdalena Bay, southern Baja California. On sand bottom from 0 to 200 fm. Most common in shallow water to 10 fm.

Remarks: Common but of no commercial importance because of small size. Serves as food for other fish, marine mammals, and seabirds. Similar to Pacific sanddab, which lacks black speckling on body. Positive identification of speckled sanddab, gulf sanddab, Pacific sanddab, and longfin sanddab require gill raker and lateral line scale counts.

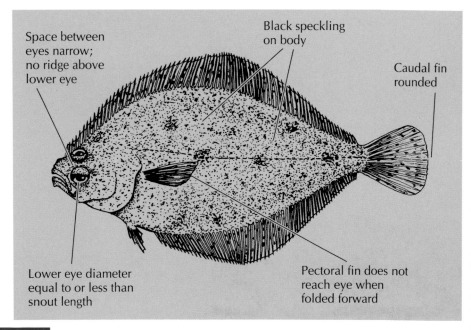

Space between eyes narrow; no ridge above lower eye

Black speckling on body

Caudal fin rounded

Lower eye diameter equal to or less than snout length

Pectoral fin does not reach eye when folded forward

Speckled sanddab, eyed side.

Speckled sanddab, blind side.

Longfin Sanddab   *Citharichthys xanthostigma*

Description: Left-eyed. Eyed side uniform dark brown with white and rust-to-orange speckles. Blind side whitish. Body shape elongate to oval. Eyed side pectoral fin is blackish with very long uppermost rays. Caudal fin rounded. Lateral line nearly straight, accessory dorsal branch absent. Mouth moderate-sized with maxillary almost to below middle of eye. Space between eyes narrow, with sharp ridge above lower eye. Anal spine absent. Gill rakers on lower limb of first arch are 10 to 12. Scale count in lateral line is 47 to 57.

Size: To 25 cm (10 inches).

Range and Habitat: Monterey Bay, California, to Costa Rica including Gulf of California. Rare north of Santa Barbara, California. On bottom to depths of 110 fm.

Remarks: Common off southern California. Distinguished from other sanddabs by very long pectoral fin on eyed side. Positive identification of longfin sanddab, gulf sanddab, Pacific sanddab, and speckled sanddab require gill raker and lateral line scale counts.

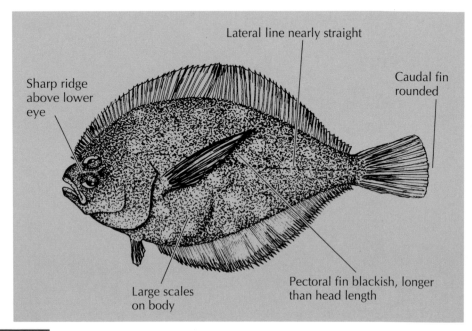

Lateral line nearly straight

Sharp ridge above lower eye

Caudal fin rounded

Large scales on body

Pectoral fin blackish, longer than head length

Longfin sanddab, eyed side.

Longfin sanddab, blind side.

Bigmouth Sole

Hippoglossina stomata

Description: Left-eyed. Eyed side brown with dark blotches and sometimes with bluish speckles. Usually five pairs of large, dark brown spots near upper and lower edges of body and one pair on the caudal peduncle. Blind side whitish. Body shape elongate to oval. Caudal fin rounded. High arch in lateral line over pectoral fin, accessory dorsal branch absent. Mouth large without noticeable teeth. Anal spine present.

Size: To 40 cm (16 inches).

Range and Habitat: Monterey Bay, California, south into the Gulf of California and including Guadalupe Island. On bottom from 16 to 75 fm.

Remarks: Flesh reported to be of high quality. Fish is uncommon and of negligible commercial importance. Similar to California halibut, which has longer jaw teeth, is larger, and has different caudal fin shape.

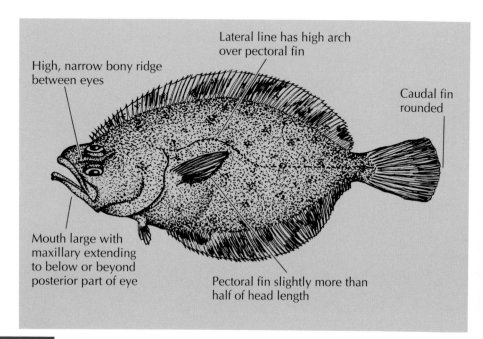

Lateral line has high arch over pectoral fin

High, narrow bony ridge between eyes

Caudal fin rounded

Mouth large with maxillary extending to below or beyond posterior part of eye

Pectoral fin slightly more than half of head length

Bigmouth sole, eyed side.

Bigmouth sole, blind side.

California Halibut   *Paralichthys californicus*

(Monterey halibut, southern halibut)

Description: Belongs to left-eyed flounder family, but can also be right-eyed (40%). Eyed side greenish or grayish brown to black; may have lighter or darker mottling. Young often have white spots. Blind side white. Scales smooth. Body shape elongate to oval. Caudal fin slightly indented near top and bottom. Lateral line with high arch, accessory dorsal branch absent. Mouth large with numerous strong teeth. Maxillary extends below or beyond posterior part of lower eye. Small eyes with wide, flat area between eyes. Anal spine absent.

Size: To 152 cm (60 inches). Reported up to 72 pounds (verified record is 61½ pounds). Average is 6 to 7 pounds.

Range and Habitat: Quillayute River, Washington, to Magdalena Bay, southern Baja California, and in Gulf of California. Sand bottom from near shore to 100 fm. Usually at depths less than 15 fm.

Remarks: An excellent food fish. Important in sport and commercial fisheries off California. Common off southern California, especially in spring. Similar to, but easily separated from bigmouth sole (which has evenly rounded tail); Pacific halibut (which has shorter maxillary); Greenland halibut (which has dark blind side); and arrowtooth flounder (which has straight lateral line).

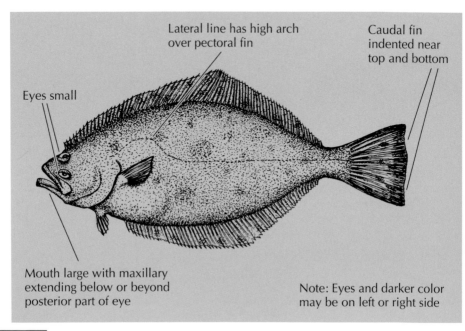

Lateral line has high arch over pectoral fin

Caudal fin indented near top and bottom

Eyes small

Mouth large with maxillary extending below or beyond posterior part of eye

Note: Eyes and darker color may be on left or right side

California halibut, eyed side. Right-eyed and left-eyed specimens.

California halibut, blind side. Left-eyed and right-eyed specimens.

California halibut, eyed side. Left-eyed specimen.

California halibut, blind side. Left-eyed specimen.

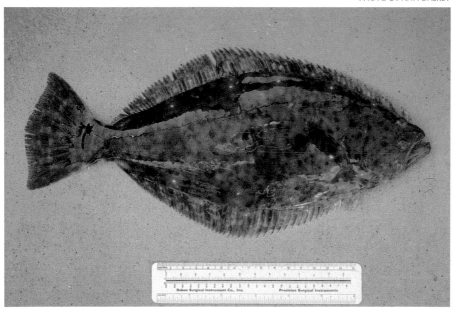

California halibut, eyed side. Right-eyed specimen.

California halibut, blind side. Right-eyed specimen.

Fantail Sole

Xystreurys liolepis

(longfin sole, true petrale)

Description: Belongs to left-eyed flounder family, but can also be right-eyed. Eyed side olive to brown with darker mottling; may have many gray or reddish-brown blotches; often has two ocelli (one behind head and one near rear of body). Blind side white. Body shape oval. Caudal fin rounded or slightly indented near top and bottom. Lateral line with high arch over pectoral fin; accessory dorsal branch absent. Mouth small with maxillary extending below about middle of lower eye. Anal spine absent.

Size: To 53 cm (21 inches). Average size is about 6 inches.

Range and Habitat: Monterey Bay, California, to central Baja California and in the northern Gulf of California. On sand or mud bottom from 2 to 44 fm. Usually buried in bottom.

Remarks: Uncommon. Rarely caught on sport fishing gear. Forms a small portion of commercial sole catch near Santa Barbara, California. Similar to bigmouth sole (which has larger mouth) and longfin sanddab (which has straight lateral line).

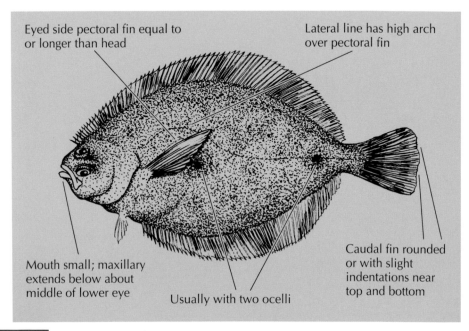

Eyed side pectoral fin equal to or longer than head

Lateral line has high arch over pectoral fin

Mouth small; maxillary extends below about middle of lower eye

Usually with two ocelli

Caudal fin rounded or with slight indentations near top and bottom

Fantail sole, eyed side. Right-eyed and left-eyed specimens.

Fantail sole, blind side. Left-eyed and right-eyed specimens.

Fantail Sole

Xystreurys liolepis

PHOTO BY ANN DALKEY

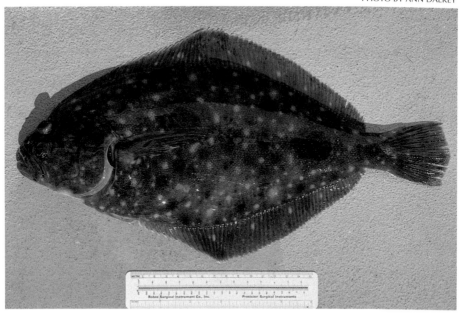

Fantail sole, eyed side. Left-eyed specimen.

PHOTO BY ANN DALKEY

Fantail sole, blind side. Left-eyed specimen.

PHOTO BY ANN DALKEY

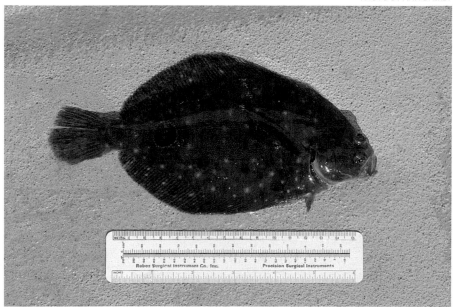

Fantail sole, eyed side. Right-eyed specimen.

PHOTO BY ANN DALKEY

Fantail sole, blind side. Right-eyed specimen.

California Tonguefish   *Symphurus atricauda*

California tongue sole

Description: Left-eyed. Eyed side light brown to gray with dark bars extending from base of dorsal and anal fins toward center of body. Blind side white. Teardrop-shaped body with pointed tail. Dorsal and anal fins fully joined at tail with no distinct caudal fin. No lateral line or accessory dorsal branch. Mouth small, twisted toward eyed side. Eyes tiny and closely set. Anal spine absent. Pectoral fins absent. One pelvic fin (on eyed side).

Size: To 21 cm (8 inches). Most less than 6 inches.

Range and Habitat: Yaquina Bay, Oregon, to Panama. On sand or mud bottom from 1 to 110 fm.

Remarks: Common off southern California; rare north of Point Conception, California. Occasionally caught by sport fishermen using small hooks. Too small to be of market value.

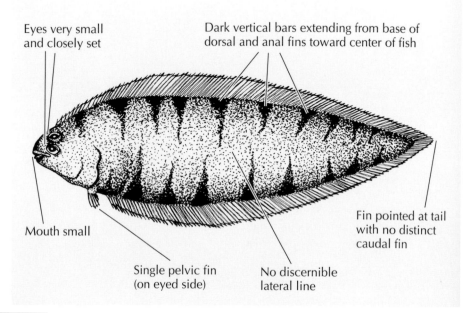

Eyes very small and closely set

Dark vertical bars extending from base of dorsal and anal fins toward center of fish

Mouth small

Fin pointed at tail with no distinct caudal fin

Single pelvic fin (on eyed side)

No discernible lateral line

PHOTO BY DONALD E. KRAMER

California tonguefish, eyed side.

PHOTO BY DONALD E. KRAMER

California tonguefish, blind side.

31

Scalyeye Plaice   *Acanthopsetta nadeshnyi*

(Nadezhny's flounder)

Description: Right-eyed. Eyed side uniform brownish. Blind side white. Body shape oval. Caudal fin rounded. Lateral line arched over pectoral fin, branch runs forward along dorsal side of head to near origin of dorsal fin. Mouth small to medium. Maxillary does not reach to below middle of lower eye. Lower eye slightly anterior to upper eye. Common name due to scales covering back of eyes. Anal spine absent.

Size: To 40 cm (16 inches).

Range and Habitat: From Sea of Japan coast along Fukui Prefecture and east coast of Korea into the Gulf of Tartary and Sea of Okhotsk and from Pacific coast of Japan along Iwate Prefecture into western Bering Sea. Occurs in deeper water than most other flatfish. On sandy bottom from 16 to 400 fm. Usually found at 30 to 40 fm.

Remarks: Taken by trawl. Low commercial value due to poor flavor caused by high oil content.

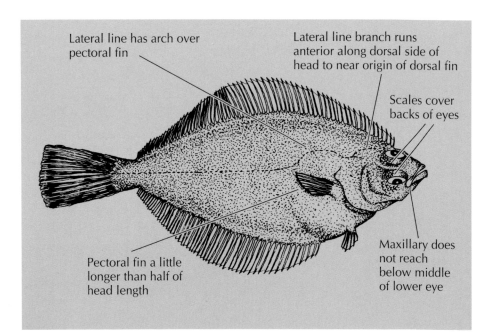

Lateral line has arch over pectoral fin

Lateral line branch runs anterior along dorsal side of head to near origin of dorsal fin

Scales cover backs of eyes

Maxillary does not reach below middle of lower eye

Pectoral fin a little longer than half of head length

PHOTO BY KUNIO AMAOKA

Scalyeye plaice, eyed side.

PHOTO BY KUNIO AMAOKA

Scalyeye plaice, blind side.

Kamchatka Flounder   *Atheresthes evermanni*

(Asiatic arrowtooth)

Description: Right-eyed. Eyed side dark brown. Blind side off-white or dirty white. Body shape elongate diamond. Caudal fin crescent-shaped. Lateral line has slight curve over pectoral fin; accessory dorsal branch absent. Mouth very large with arrow-shaped teeth. Maxillary extends to below or beyond posterior margin of lower eye. No fang-like teeth on vomer (bone in roof of mouth). Upper eye usually below dorsal ridge (not visible from blind side). Anal spine absent. Preopercle C-shaped (not angular). Anterior nostril on blind side has large flap. Dorsal fin origin at or anterior to middle of eye. Deciduous scales.

Size: To 84 cm (33 inches).

Range and Habitat: In Sea of Japan and Sea of Okhotsk north to Gulf of Anadyr. In Bering Sea east to Bristol Bay; north and south of the Aleutian Islands east to Shelikof Strait. On sand or mud bottoms from 14 to 600 fm. Most reported between 27 and 270 fm.

Remarks: Very similar to arrowtooth flounder, which has different upper eye position. Similar to Greenland halibut, which has L-shaped (angular) preopercle. Can be distinguished from arrowtooth flounder by gill raker counts.

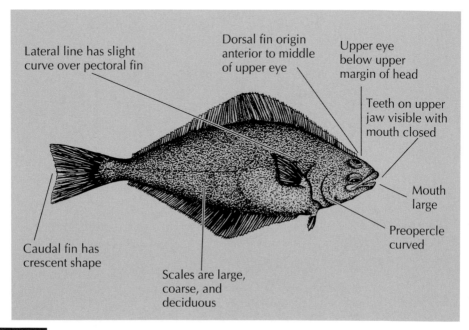

Lateral line has slight curve over pectoral fin

Dorsal fin origin anterior to middle of upper eye

Upper eye below upper margin of head

Teeth on upper jaw visible with mouth closed

Mouth large

Preopercle curved

Caudal fin has crescent shape

Scales are large, coarse, and deciduous

PHOTO BY DONALD E. KRAMER

Kamchatka flounder, eyed side.

PHOTO BY DONALD E. KRAMER

Kamchatka flounder, blind side.

Arrowtooth Flounder　　*Atheresthes stomias*

(longjaw flounder, French sole, turbot)

Description: Right-eyed. Eyed side uniform dark grayish brown to olive brown. Blind side dirty white to light gray. Scales darker at edges. Body shape elongate diamond. Caudal fin crescent-shaped. Lateral line nearly straight with slight curve over pectoral fin; accessory dorsal branch absent. Mouth very large with two rows of sharp arrow-shaped teeth. Maxillary extends below or beyond posterior margin of lower eye. No fang-like teeth on vomer (bone in roof of mouth). Left eye on dorsal ridge (visible from blind side). Anal spine absent. Preopercle C-shaped (not angular). Anterior nostril on blind side has small flap. Dorsal fin origin at middle of eye.

Size: To 86 cm (34 inches) and up to 17 pounds. Often large, and females are bigger than males.

Range and Habitat: Eastern Bering Sea to San Pedro, southern California. (San Pedro record may have been a slender sole.) North and south of Alaska Peninsula and Aleutians. One specimen reported from Chukchi Sea. On soft bottoms from 10 to 400 fm. Most common at 150 to 220 fm.

Remarks: Common in waters of Alaska through Oregon. Very abundant in the Gulf of Alaska. Taken primarily in trawls. Not of high commercial value due to poor flesh quality. Used traditionally as animal feed, but human consumption increasing.

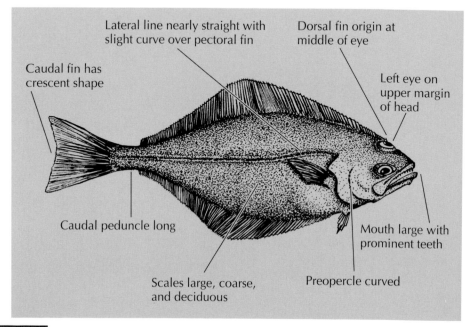

Lateral line nearly straight with slight curve over pectoral fin

Dorsal fin origin at middle of eye

Caudal fin has crescent shape

Left eye on upper margin of head

Caudal peduncle long

Scales large, coarse, and deciduous

Preopercle curved

Mouth large with prominent teeth

PHOTO BY DONALD E. KRAMER

Arrowtooth flounder, eyed side.

PHOTO BY DONALD E. KRAMER

Arrowtooth flounder, blind side.

Roughscale Sole
Clidoderma asperrimum

Description: Right-eyed. Eyed side uniform brown. Blind side gray. Body shape round. Caudal fin rounded. Lateral line has low arch over pectoral fin; short lateral line branch over left eye; accessory dorsal branch absent. Mouth small. Maxillary extends below anterior margin of lower eye. Eyes large with lower eye slightly anterior. Anal spine absent. Six or more irregular rows of rough, scaly plates (tubercles) on eyed side. Blind side smooth.

Size: To 55 cm (22 inches).

Range and Habitat: Yellow Sea and Sea of Japan north into Sea of Okhotsk. Bering Sea south to Punta Gorda, Mendocino County, California. In eastern Pacific on mud bottoms at 185 to 190 fm.

Remarks: Common off Japan, but rare in eastern Pacific waters.

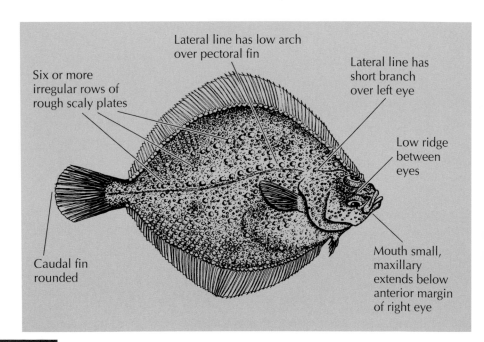

Lateral line has low arch over pectoral fin

Six or more irregular rows of rough scaly plates

Lateral line has short branch over left eye

Low ridge between eyes

Caudal fin rounded

Mouth small, maxillary extends below anterior margin of right eye

PHOTO BY DONALD E. KRAMER

Roughscale sole, eyed side.

PHOTO BY DONALD E. KRAMER

Roughscale sole, blind side.

Description: Right-eyed. Both sides colored. Eyed side dark gray to reddish brown, darker on upper and lower thirds of body; broad bluish blotches can be seen in fresh specimens. Blind side dusky gray to brown. Body shape oval with small, rounded caudal fin. Lateral line nearly straight with very low arch over pectoral fin; accessory dorsal branch absent. Mouth small with prominent black lips. Maxillary extends to below anterior part of right eye. Teeth moderately developed on both sides of both jaws. Eyes large. High ridge between eyes. Anal spine absent.

Size: To 47 cm (inches).

Range and Habitat: Northern Japan through Gulf of Alaska to California-Mexico border. A deepwater species found on mud bottoms from 185 to 750 fm; most are deeper than 350 fm.

Remarks: Extremely flabby flatfish of no commercial importance. Similar to Dover sole, which has a more slender body and teeth mostly on blind side.

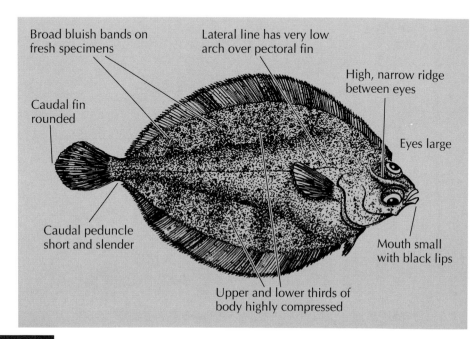

Broad bluish bands on fresh specimens

Lateral line has very low arch over pectoral fin

High, narrow ridge between eyes

Caudal fin rounded

Eyes large

Caudal peduncle short and slender

Mouth small with black lips

Upper and lower thirds of body highly compressed

Deepsea sole, eyed side.

Deepsea sole, blind side.

Slender Sole

Eopsetta exilis

(rough sole)

Formerly Lyopsetta exilis

Description: Right-eyed. Eyed side pale olive brown to reddish brown with black speckling on edges of fins. Blind side whitish to pale yellow or orange. Body slender, elongate. Caudal fin rounded or pointed. Pectoral fins small, narrow; fins dusky, but dorsal and ventral may be pale at edges. Lateral line nearly straight; accessory dorsal branch absent. Mouth medium to large with maxillary extending to or almost to middle of lower eye. Teeth on both sides of both jaws with two rows on upper jaw. Eyes large; upper eye at top of head. High ridge running from between eyes to lateral line. Anal spine strong, sharp. Deciduous scales large, prominent (or scale pockets on trawled specimens).

Size: To 35 cm (14 inches). Small, most less than 10 inches; average size about 8 inches.

Range and Habitat: From North Albatross Bank off Alaska (east of Kodiak Island), to Cedros Island, central Baja California. One record in Bering Sea. On muddy or silty bottoms. From 5 to 437 fm; mostly at 40 to 110 fm during summer.

Remarks: Common. Excellent flavor, but too small to be of commercial importance.

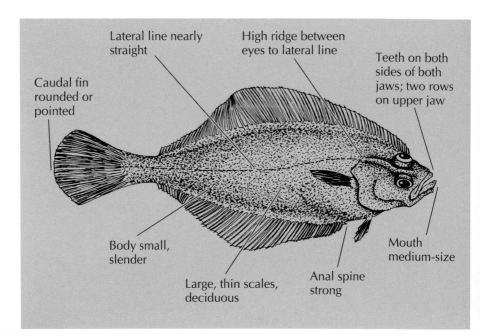

Lateral line nearly straight

High ridge between eyes to lateral line

Teeth on both sides of both jaws; two rows on upper jaw

Caudal fin rounded or pointed

Body small, slender

Large, thin scales, deciduous

Anal spine strong

Mouth medium-size

PHOTO BY DOUGLAS F. MARKLE

Slender sole, eyed side.

PHOTO BY BARRY E. BRACKEN

Slender sole, blind side.

Petrale Sole

Eopsetta jordani

(brill, California sole, roundnosed sole)

Description: Right-eyed. Eyed side uniform light to dark brown. Blind side white, sometimes with pink traces. Body shape oval to round. Caudal fin longest in middle and slightly indented near edges. Lateral line with low curve over pectoral fin; accessory dorsal branch absent. Mouth large. Maxillary extends to below or slightly beyond middle of lower eye. Upper jaw with two rows of small, arrow-shaped teeth; one row of teeth on lower jaw. Posterior edge of lower jaw rounded. Eyes medium-sized with broad space between them. Anal spine strong.

Size: To 70 cm (28 inches) and 8 pounds. Average size in trawl catch is about 1 to 2 pounds.

Range and Habitat: Bering Sea and Aleutian Islands through Gulf of Alaska to Coronado Islands, northern Baja California. On sand and mud bottoms from 10 to 300 fm. Most abundant at 30 to 70 fm from April through October and at 150 to 250 fm during winter.

Remarks: Important commercially because of good size and excellent quality. Most caught by trawl and marketed as fresh or frozen fillets. Similar to flathead sole and Bering flounder which have one row of teeth on upper jaw.

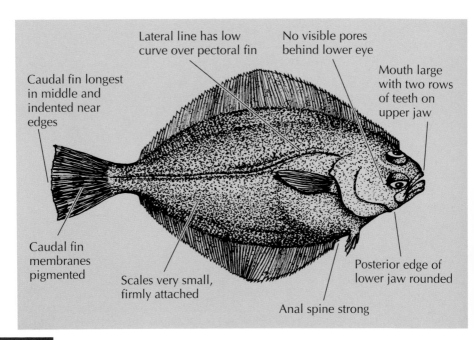

Lateral line has low curve over pectoral fin

No visible pores behind lower eye

Caudal fin longest in middle and indented near edges

Mouth large with two rows of teeth on upper jaw

Caudal fin membranes pigmented

Scales very small, firmly attached

Posterior edge of lower jaw rounded

Anal spine strong

PHOTO BY WILLIAM H. BARSS

Petrale sole, eyed side.

PHOTO BY DONALD E. KRAMER

Petrale sole, blind side.

Rex Sole

Errex zachirus

(longfinned sole, witch sole) *Formerly Glyptocephalus zachirus*

Description: Right-eyed. Eyed side uniform light brown to gray. Edges of dorsal and ventral fins dark or dusky. Pectoral fin on eyed side very long and mostly black. Blind side off-white to dusky. Body elongate. Caudal fin rounded with rays longest in center, forming a broad V. Lateral line straight. Mouth very small. Maxillary extends to below anterior edge of lower eye. Snout rounded. Eyes large with ridge between them. Anal spine strong. Scales small.

Size: To 61 cm (24 inches). Average size about 10 inches and ½ pound.

Range and Habitat: Bering Sea and Aleutian Islands to Cedros Island, central Baja California. Widely distributed on sand and mud bottoms from 0 to 465 fm. Most abundant at about 100 to 250 fm.

Remarks: Abundant and an excellent food fish. Not heavily used commercially because of small size and thin body. Has been used in the past for animal feed, but use as a market species is growing (frozen head off and gutted).

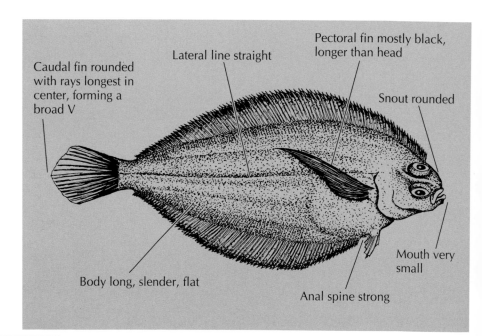

Caudal fin rounded with rays longest in center, forming a broad V

Lateral line straight

Pectoral fin mostly black, longer than head

Snout rounded

Body long, slender, flat

Anal spine strong

Mouth very small

Rex sole, eyed side.

Rex sole, blind side.

Korean Flounder

Glyptocephalus stelleri

(Steller's smallmouth flounder)

Description: Right-eyed. Eyed side grayish brown. Blind side gray. Body shape elongate to oval. Caudal fin rounded. Lateral line nearly straight. Mouth small with teeth on both sides of both jaws. Maxillary extends to below anterior part of lower eye. High, narrow ridge between eyes is not scaled, but eyelids are. Anal spine present.

Size: To 60 cm (24 inches). Most common size in catches is 15 to 17 inches and 1 to 2 pounds.

Range and Habitat: From Sea of Japan into Sea of Okhotsk and from Pacific coast of Chiba Prefecture of Japan into Bering Sea. On sand and mud bottoms from 10 to 137 fm.

Remarks: Taken by trawl. A fine food fish with very good flavor. Similar to rex sole, which has much longer pectoral fin on eyed side.

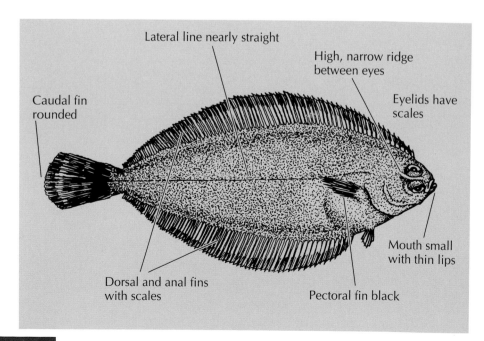

Lateral line nearly straight

High, narrow ridge between eyes

Caudal fin rounded

Eyelids have scales

Dorsal and anal fins with scales

Pectoral fin black

Mouth small with thin lips

Korean flounder, eyed side.

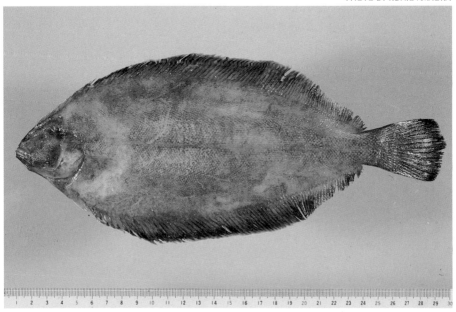

Korean flounder, blind side.

Flathead Sole   *Hippoglossoides elassodon*

(cigarette paper, paper sole)

Description: Right-eyed. Eyed side dark olive brown to reddish gray-brown, sometimes with dusky blotches. Blind side with white and translucent areas; dorsal and anal fins have dusky blotches. Body shape oval and very flat. Caudal fin angular with longest rays at center. Lateral line nearly straight with low arch over pectoral fin; accessory dorsal branch absent but an anterior branch runs almost to rear edge of upper eye. Mouth medium to large. Maxillary extends to below middle of lower eye. Both jaws have one row of sharp, conical teeth. Eyes large with narrow ridge and 1–2 rows of scales between them. Anal spine strong. Pores below and behind lower eye may be hard to see.

Size: To 56 cm (22 inches).

Range and Habitat: Kurile Islands north to Gulf of Anadyr. In Chukchi Sea, Bering Sea, and along Aleutian Islands south to Monterey, California. On silty or muddy bottoms from 0 to 575 fm. Most common from 55 to 135 fm.

Remarks: Good food fish, but body is thin. Of limited commercial use in past, but becoming more important. Very similar to Bering flounder. Petrale sole is similar, but upper jaw has two rows of teeth and lower jaw has rounded rear edge.

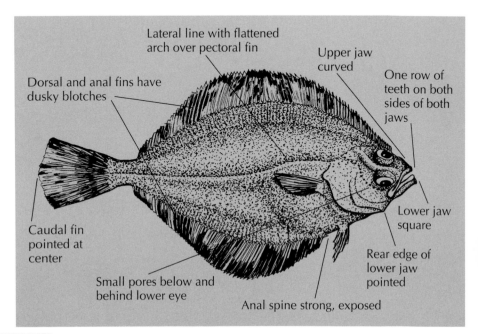

Lateral line with flattened arch over pectoral fin

Upper jaw curved

One row of teeth on both sides of both jaws

Dorsal and anal fins have dusky blotches

Lower jaw square

Caudal fin pointed at center

Rear edge of lower jaw pointed

Small pores below and behind lower eye

Anal spine strong, exposed

Flathead sole, eyed side.

Flathead sole, blind side.

51

Bering Flounder　　　*Hippoglossoides robustus*

Description: Right-eyed. Eyed side reddish brown to dark grayish brown. Blind side white. Body shape elongate to oval. Caudal fin rounded. Caudal fin membranes clear, but may have dark smudges. Lateral line has low arch over pectoral fin; accessory dorsal branch absent, but anterior branch present. Mouth large with maxillary extending to below or past middle of lower eye. Upper jaw has one row of teeth. Rear of lower jaw pointed. Space between eyes flat with two rows of scales. Anal spine present. Pores ventral and posterior to lower eye may be hard to see.

Size: To 30 cm (12 inches).

Range and Habitat: From Hokkaido north into Sea of Okhotsk. From Cape Lisburne in Chukchi Sea to north side of Alaska Peninsula and Aleutian Islands. Reported from 10 to 232 fm; usually found in shallow water above 80 fm.

Remarks: Very similar to flathead sole, but has more elongate body, smaller eyes, wider space between eyes, greater curve in lateral line, and lacks raised ridge between eyes.

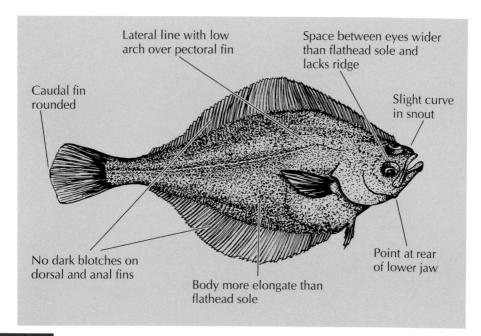

Lateral line with low arch over pectoral fin

Space between eyes wider than flathead sole and lacks ridge

Caudal fin rounded

Slight curve in snout

No dark blotches on dorsal and anal fins

Body more elongate than flathead sole

Point at rear of lower jaw

Bering flounder, eyed side.

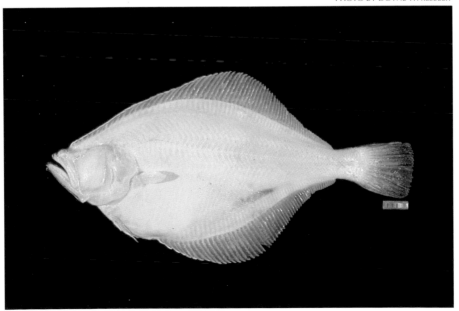

Bering flounder, blind side.

Pacific Halibut
Hippoglossus stenolepis

(northern halibut, right halibut)

Description: Almost always right-eyed. Eyed side greenish brown to dark brown or black with lighter blotches. Blind side white to milky white. Body large and stout with elongate diamond shape. Caudal fin has crescent shape often indented near edges (double truncate). Lateral line has high arch over pectoral fin, accessory dorsal branch absent. Mouth medium to large with two rows of teeth on upper jaw and one row on lower jaw. Maxillary reaches to below middle of lower eye. Area between eyes flat to slightly concave. Anal spine present. Scales small and smooth on both sides of body.

Size: To 267 cm (105 inches) and 500 pounds. There are unverified reports of fish over 9 feet and 700 pounds. Average size in commercial catch is 30 to 40 pounds.

Range and Habitat: Sea of Japan and Sea of Okhotsk north to Gulf of Anadyr. Bering Sea south to Point Camalu, northern Baja California. Found from 3 to 600 fm. Mostly in 15 to 150 fm in summer, but deeper in winter.

Remarks: Abundant. Largest, most valuable flatfish in the northeast Pacific; important as commercial and sport fish. Similar to California halibut, which has larger mouth and less indented tail.

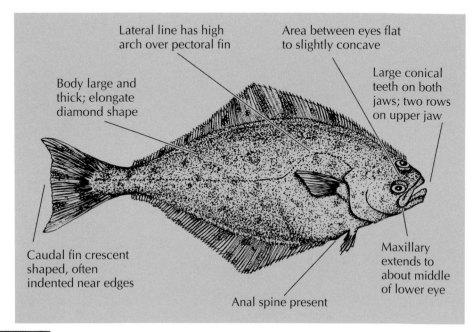

Lateral line has high arch over pectoral fin

Area between eyes flat to slightly concave

Body large and thick; elongate diamond shape

Large conical teeth on both jaws; two rows on upper jaw

Caudal fin crescent shaped, often indented near edges

Maxillary extends to about middle of lower eye

Anal spine present

Pacific halibut, eyed side.

Pacific halibut, blind side.

Diamond Turbot

Hypsopsetta guttulata

(diamond flounder)

Description: Right-eyed. Eyed side dark greenish or grayish brown with light bluish spotting. Blind side bright porcelain white with bright yellow around mouth and edge of head. Deep body with diamond shape. Caudal fin rounded. Lateral line nearly straight with slight curve over pectoral fin; long accessory dorsal branch extends more than halfway to caudal fin. Mouth small. Maxillary extends to below anterior edge of lower eye. Teeth small; very few on eyed side. Low ridge between eyes. Anal spine present.

Size: To 46 cm (18 inches) and 4 pounds. Average weight for sport catch is a little over 1 pound.

Range and Habitat: Cape Mendocino, California, to Cape San Lucas, Baja California. Isolated population in Gulf of California. On mud and sand bottoms from 0 to 25 fm. Most common in 1 to 10 fm. Often found in bays or sloughs and up rivers in brackish to fresh waters.

Remarks: Highly regarded as food because of thick body and fine flavor. Sometimes has slight iodine flavor. Other turbots in its range, spotted turbot and hornyhead turbot, have four or more anterior dorsal fin rays extending down blind side.

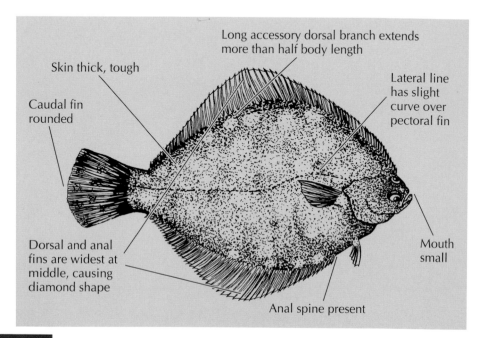

Skin thick, tough

Long accessory dorsal branch extends more than half body length

Lateral line has slight curve over pectoral fin

Caudal fin rounded

Dorsal and anal fins are widest at middle, causing diamond shape

Mouth small

Anal spine present

Diamond turbot, eyed side.

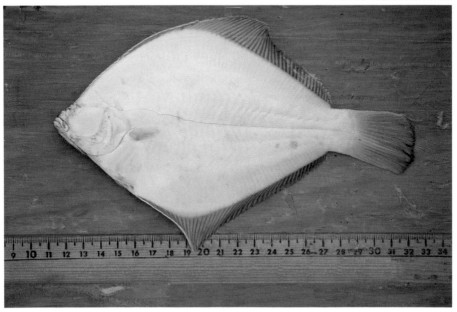

Diamond turbot, blind side.

Forkline Sole

Inopsetta ischyra

(bastard sole, hybrid sole)

Description: Right-eyed. Eyed side brown to olive brown and mottled with lighter and darker areas. Dorsal and anal fins with faint dusky bars. Blind side creamy white. Body diamond-shaped. Caudal fin varies from rounded to almost straight. Lateral line extends onto caudal fin; short, forked accessory dorsal branch does not extend past gill cover. Mouth small with maxillary extending below anterior edge of lower eye. Prominent rugose ridge runs from between eyes posterior to upper eye. Anal spine sharp. Rough scales on both sides of body and on dorsal and anal fins.

Size: To 46 cm (18 inches).

Range and Habitat: Bering Sea to San Francisco, California. Rare outside of Puget Sound. On soft bottom to depths of 360 fm.

Remarks: May be a cross between English sole and starry flounder, although rock sole has been suggested as a possible parent; quite variable, possibly due to back crosses (see Hart 1973). Distinguishable from English sole, which has no bars on fins, longer lateral line branch, and more pointed snout; and from starry flounder, which has bars on caudal fin, more distinct bars in dorsal and anal fins, and star-shaped tubercles on body.

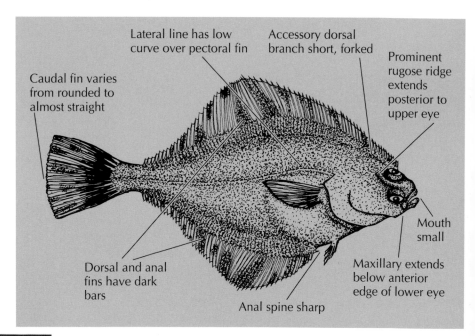

Lateral line has low curve over pectoral fin

Accessory dorsal branch short, forked

Prominent rugose ridge extends posterior to upper eye

Caudal fin varies from rounded to almost straight

Dorsal and anal fins have dark bars

Anal spine sharp

Maxillary extends below anterior edge of lower eye

Mouth small

Forkline sole, eyed side.

Forkline sole, blind side.

Dover Sole
Microstomus pacificus

(shortfinned sole, slime sole, slippery sole)

Description: Right-eyed. Eyed side brown or grayish brown; may be mottled with darker spots. Fins blackish toward edges. Blind side smudgy off-white to dark brownish gray. Body elongate with very small scales. Caudal fin rounded. Lateral line nearly straight with short, unconnected branch near top of head which is difficult to see; accessory dorsal branch absent. Mouth very small. Maxillary extends to below anterior of lower eye. Teeth mostly on blind side; teeth flat and like incisors. Eyes large and bulging, with upper eye posterior to lower eye. Space between eyes convex. Anal spine absent. Soft, flabby body is slippery, because of large amounts of slime.

Size: To 76 cm (30 inches) and up to 10 pounds. Average size in trawl catch is about 1 pound.

Range and Habitat: Bering Sea and eastern Aleutian Islands to San Cristobal Bay, Baja California. On mud or sand bottoms from 5 to 750 fm. Commercial catches are from 40 to 550 fm.

Remarks: Common and widely distributed. Important commercially; marketed as fillets. Good flavor and good keeping qualities. Flesh quality reported to be poorer for fish caught below 300 fm.

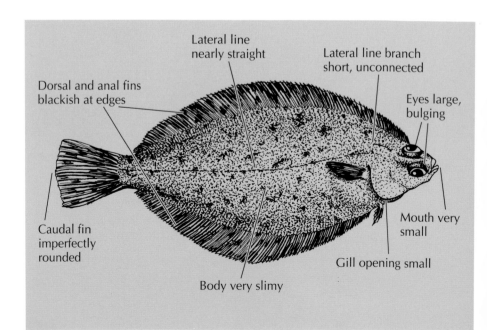

Lateral line nearly straight

Lateral line branch short, unconnected

Dorsal and anal fins blackish at edges

Eyes large, bulging

Caudal fin imperfectly rounded

Mouth very small

Gill opening small

Body very slimy

Dover sole, eyed side.

Dover sole, blind side.

Starry Flounder

Platichthys stellatus

(diamond back, emerywheel, grindstone)

Description: Belongs to right-eyed flounder family, but can also be left-eyed. Eyed side olive to dark brown or almost black. Unpaired fins white to yellow to orange with black bars. Blind side white to creamy white. Body shape oval. Caudal fin nearly square or slightly rounded. Lateral line with slight curve over pectoral fin; accessory dorsal branch absent. Mouth small. Maxillary extends below anterior part of lower eye. Eyes small with lower eye anterior to upper eye. Space between eyes flat. Head slender, pointed. Anal spine strong. Scattered rough tubercles (star-like scales) on eyed side.

Size: To 91 cm (36 inches) and 20 pounds. Usual size is 12 to 14 inches.

Range and Habitat: In Sea of Japan and Sea of Okhotsk. From Chukchi Sea, Bering Sea, and Aleutian Islands south to Los Angeles Harbor, California. On mud, sand, or gravel bottoms from 0 to 205 fm; most occur above 80 fm. Usually found near shore. Often enters brackish or fresh water, and young fish are often intertidal.

Remarks: Common. Important sport fish. Highly regarded as food fish, but has moderate commercial value. Processing difficult due to rough skin, and needs to be deep skinned to remove unappealing, dark fat layer.

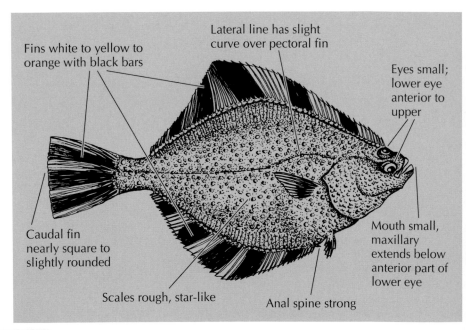

Fins white to yellow to orange with black bars

Lateral line has slight curve over pectoral fin

Eyes small; lower eye anterior to upper

Caudal fin nearly square to slightly rounded

Scales rough, star-like

Anal spine strong

Mouth small, maxillary extends below anterior part of lower eye

PHOTO BY DONALD E. KRAMER

Starry flounder, eyed side. Left-eyed and right-eyed specimens.

PHOTO BY DONALD E. KRAMER

Starry flounder, blind side. Left-eyed and right-eyed specimens.

Starry Flounder   *Platichthys stellatus*

Starry flounder, eyed side. Right-eyed specimen.

Starry flounder, blind side. Right-eyed specimen.

Starry flounder, eyed side. Left-eyed specimen.

Starry flounder, blind side. Left-eyed specimen.

Yellowfin Sole

Pleuronectes asper

(Alaska dab, muddab, northern sole)

Formerly Limanda aspera

Description: Right-eyed. Eyed side olive to brown with dark mottling. Dorsal and anal fins have faint dark bars, and a narrow black line at base. Blind side snowy white. Fins yellowish on both sides of body. Body shape round. Caudal fin rounded at edges. Lateral line has high arch over pectoral fin; accessory dorsal branch absent. Mouth small. Maxillary barely reaches below anterior edge of lower eye. Teeth mainly on blind side. Eyes moderately large and almost side-by-side. Space between eyes narrow. Anal spine thin, sharp, exposed. Scales rough, on both sides of body. Scales on rays of median fins.

Size: To 48 cm (19 inches). Average size is 13 inches and ½ to 1 pound.

Range and Habitat: In Sea of Japan and Sea of Okhotsk. From Cape Lisburne, Chukchi Sea, through Bering Sea and Aleutians to Barkley Sound, Vancouver Island. Very rare in British Columbia. On sandy to hard bottoms from 1 to 328 fm. Most common in shallow water to 50 fm.

Remarks: Excellent food fish. Dominant flatfish in Bering Sea. Distinguished from butter sole, forkline sole, and rock sole, which have a dorsal accessory branch to the lateral line. Similar to Sakhalin sole, which lacks black line at base of fins.

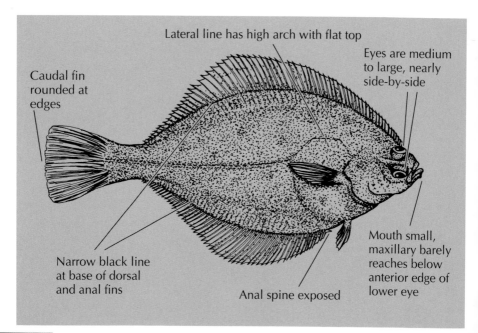

Lateral line has high arch with flat top

Eyes are medium to large, nearly side-by-side

Caudal fin rounded at edges

Narrow black line at base of dorsal and anal fins

Anal spine exposed

Mouth small, maxillary barely reaches below anterior edge of lower eye

PHOTO BY DONALD E. KRAMER

Yellowfin sole, eyed side.

PHOTO BY DONALD E. KRAMER

Yellowfin sole, blind side.

Rock Sole

Pleuronectes bilineatus

(broadfin sole, roughscale sole, two-lined flounder)

Formerly Lepidopsetta bilineata

Description: Right-eyed. Eyed side gray to olive to dark brown or black, mottled with lighter or darker shades, sometimes spotted with yellow or red. Dorsal and anal fins have dark blotches or bars; fins may be yellowish near tail. Body thick, oval to round. Caudal fin rounded or in shape of a broad V. Lateral line has high arch with flat top; accessory dorsal branch short. Mouth small with fleshy lips. Maxillary extends below anterior edge of eye. Teeth more strongly developed on blind side. Eyes small. Anal spine strong. Scales rough, tuberculate on eyed side.

Size: To 61 cm (24 inches) and 6 pounds. Weight is usually between 1 and 1½ pounds.

Range and Habitat: In Sea of Japan and Sea of Okhotsk. From Bering Strait south to Tanner Bank off southern California. On rocky, pebbly, or sandy bottoms from 0 to 315 fm. Most are caught in 20 to 40 fm.

Remarks: Abundant. Good food fish. Important commercial species in Canada and of increasing importance in Alaska, particularly for fish with roe. Similar to butter sole, which has a low lateral line arch and longer accessory dorsal branch.

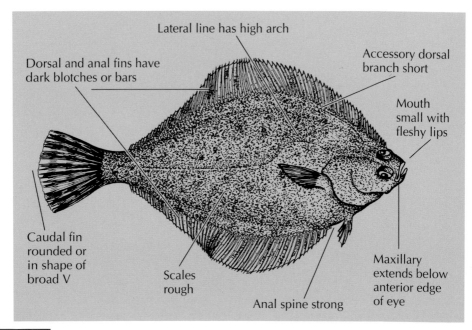

Lateral line has high arch

Dorsal and anal fins have dark blotches or bars

Accessory dorsal branch short

Mouth small with fleshy lips

Caudal fin rounded or in shape of broad V

Scales rough

Anal spine strong

Maxillary extends below anterior edge of eye

PHOTO BY DONALD E. KRAMER

Rock sole, eyed side.

PHOTO BY BARRY E. BRACKEN

Rock sole, blind side.

Arctic Flounder

Pleuronectes glacialis

(polar flounder)

Formerly Liopsetta glacialis

Description: Right-eyed. Eyed side brownish with dark markings. Dorsal and anal fins spotted. Blind side chalky white to lime green. Body elongate. Caudal fin rounded. Lateral line almost straight with slight curve over pectoral fin; accessory dorsal branch absent, but lateral line is forked at head end to form anterior branch and ventral branch. Mouth medium-sized. Maxillary reaches to anterior edge of lower eye. Teeth primarily on blind side. Prominent rugose ridge runs posterior to eyes. Scales small. Anal spine present.

Size: To 25 cm (10 inches).

Range and Habitat: White Sea east through Beaufort Sea to Bathurst Inlet, Northwest Territories. South into Bering Sea and Sea of Okhotsk. Shallow water species found to 50 fm.

Remarks: A northern species. Sometimes enters fresh water.

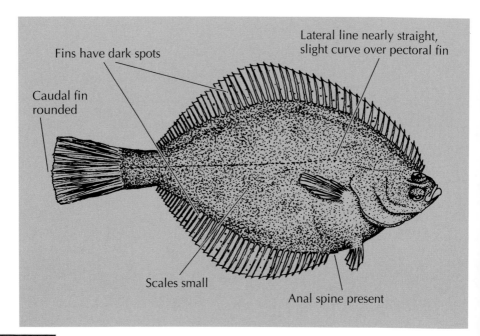

Fins have dark spots

Lateral line nearly straight, slight curve over pectoral fin

Caudal fin rounded

Scales small

Anal spine present

Arctic flounder, eyed side.

Arctic flounder, blind side.

Butter Sole
Pleuronectes isolepis

(Bellingham sole, scalyfin sole, Skidegate sole)

Formerly Isopsetta isolepis

Description: Right-eyed. Eyed side light to dark brown or grayish brown with yellow or green mottling. Blind side white. Dorsal and anal fins edged with bright lemon yellow. Body shape oval. Caudal fin rounded to broad V-shape. Lateral line has low arch over pectoral fin; long accessory dorsal branch extends past gill cover. Mouth small. Teeth blunt, strongest on blind side. Maxillary extends below anterior part of eye. Eyes small. Space between eyes flat, narrow. Anal spine strong. Scales on eyed side rough, extend onto fin rays.

Size: To 55 cm (22 inches). Usually under 12 inches with average about 8 inches.

Range and Habitat: Southern Bering Sea and Aleutian Islands south to Ventura, southern California. On muddy or silty bottoms from 0 to 232 fm. Common in shallow water; few deeper than 50 fm.

Remarks: Good food fish with excellent flavor. Low commercial value because of small size and rough scales. Similar to rock sole, which has higher arch in lateral line and shorter accessory dorsal branch.

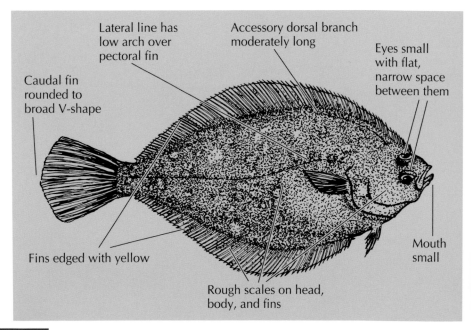

Lateral line has low arch over pectoral fin

Accessory dorsal branch moderately long

Eyes small with flat, narrow space between them

Caudal fin rounded to broad V-shape

Fins edged with yellow

Rough scales on head, body, and fins

Mouth small

Butter sole, eyed side.

Butter sole, blind side.

Dark Flounder

Pleuronectes obscurus

Formerly Liopsetta obscura

Description: Right-eyed. Eyed side uniform dark brown. Blind side yellowish white. Dorsal and anal fins have indistinct dark bars. Caudal fin rounded and sometimes tipped with yellow. Lateral line has low but distinct arch over pectoral fin. Accessory dorsal branch absent. Maxillary reaches below anterior edge of eye. Teeth large and blunt, primarily on blind side. Space between eyes has scales. Anal spine present.

Size: To 40 cm (16 inches).

Range and Habitat: From Yellow Sea and Sea of Japan into Sea of Okhotsk. Reported from Alaskan waters, but that record is doubtful. Can live in brackish water.

Remarks: An Asian species that rarely, if ever, strays into Alaskan waters.

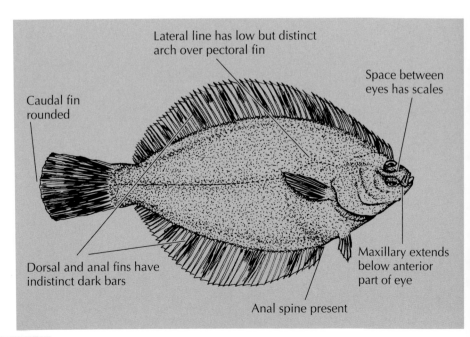

Lateral line has low but distinct arch over pectoral fin

Space between eyes has scales

Caudal fin rounded

Dorsal and anal fins have indistinct dark bars

Anal spine present

Maxillary extends below anterior part of eye

Dark flounder, eyed side.

Dark flounder, blind side.

Longhead Dab

Pleuronectes proboscideus

(longnosed flounder, longsnouted flounder)

Formerly Limanda proboscidea

Description: Right-eyed. Eyed side olive brown to grayish brown with small, indistinct, whitish spots. Blind side lemon yellow, brighter at upper and lower edges of body. Body shape elongate to oval. Caudal fin slightly rounded. Head long, pointed. Dorsal profile concave above eyes. Lateral line has high, prominent arch; accessory dorsal branch absent. Mouth small. Maxillary barely reaches to below anterior edge of lower eye. Teeth very small, primarily on blind side. Rugose ridge posterior to eyes. Anal spine present.

Size: To 41 cm (16 inches).

Range and Habitat: From Peter the Great Bay north into Sea of Okhotsk. From Cape Krusenstern, Chukchi Sea, south into Bering Sea. Along north side of Alaska Peninsula to Bristol Bay. Taken from 5 to 68 fm. Most found above 50 fm.

Remarks: Distinguished from yellowfin sole by shape of head and color of blind side. The Alaska plaice also has a yellow blind side but has 3 to 7 prominent bony cones posterior to the upper eye, not present in the longhead dab.

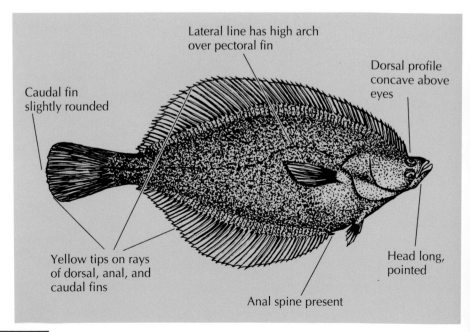

Lateral line has high arch over pectoral fin

Dorsal profile concave above eyes

Caudal fin slightly rounded

Yellow tips on rays of dorsal, anal, and caudal fins

Anal spine present

Head long, pointed

Longhead dab, eyed side.

Longhead dab, blind side.

(lemon sole, yellow-bellied flounder)

Description: Right-eyed. Eyed side uniform olive green to brown to black. Blind side yellow. Round to oval body shape. Dorsal head profile distinctly convex. Caudal fin rounded. Lateral line has moderate arch over pectoral fin; accessory dorsal branch absent, but short lateral line branch runs anterior along top of head. Small to medium-sized mouth. Maxillary extends below anterior part of lower eye. Teeth primarily on blind side. Ridge anterior to upper eye broken into 3 to 7 prominent bony cones. Anal spine present.

Size: To 60 cm (24 inches) and 3 pounds. Average size caught is about 15 inches and 1½ pounds.

Range and Habitat: From Peter the Great Bay north into the Sea of Okhotsk. From Point Hope, Chukchi Sea, south through the Bering Sea to Port Camden, southeast Alaska. One report from Washington cannot be verified.

Remarks: An incidental catch in Bering Sea trawl fisheries. Resembles English sole, which has white blind side and lacks bony cones behind upper eye, and has a more pointed head shape. Longhead dab has a yellow blind side but like English sole, lacks the bony cones and has a more pointed head shape.

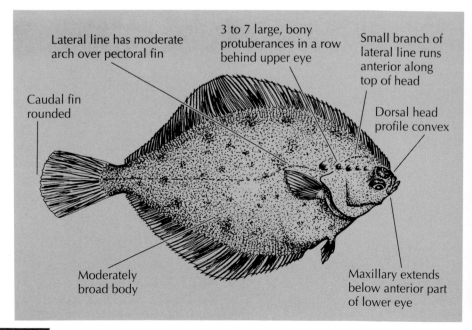

Lateral line has moderate arch over pectoral fin

3 to 7 large, bony protuberances in a row behind upper eye

Small branch of lateral line runs anterior along top of head

Caudal fin rounded

Dorsal head profile convex

Moderately broad body

Maxillary extends below anterior part of lower eye

Alaska plaice, eyed side.

Alaska plaice, blind side.

Sakhalin Sole

Pleuronectes sakhalinensis

(Sakhalin flounder)

Formerly Limanda sakhalinensis

Description: Right-eyed. Eyed side uniform medium to dark brown. Blind side white. Fins brownish. Body shape elongate to oval. Caudal fin rounded. Lateral line has medium to high arch over pectoral fin; accessory dorsal branch absent. Mouth small. Maxillary extends below anterior edge of lower eye. Space between eyes convex. Anal spine present. Origin of dorsal fin is over middle of upper eye.

Size: To 35 cm (14 inches).

Range and Habitat: Sea of Okhotsk through western and central Bering Sea at least as far east as the Pribilof Islands. Most common in western Bering Sea. Rare in eastern Bering Sea. Found from 11 to 41 fm.

Remarks: Very similar to yellowfin sole (which has rounder body, darker color, higher arch in lateral line, and a narrow black line on eyed side at base of dorsal and anal fins). Similar to rock sole (which is darker and has an accessory dorsal branch of the lateral line).

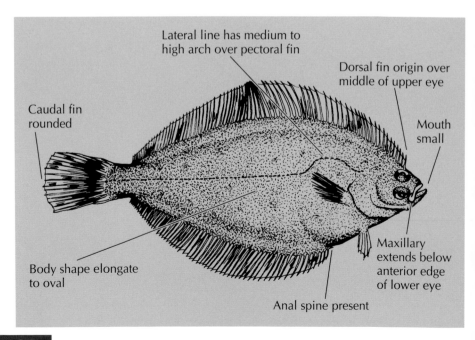

Lateral line has medium to high arch over pectoral fin

Dorsal fin origin over middle of upper eye

Caudal fin rounded

Mouth small

Maxillary extends below anterior edge of lower eye

Body shape elongate to oval

Anal spine present

PHOTO BY DONALD E. KRAMER

Sakhalin sole, eyed side.

PHOTO BY DONALD E. KRAMER

Sakhalin sole, blind side.

English Sole

Pleuronectes vetulus

(California sole, lemon sole, pointed nose sole)

Formerly Parophrys vetulus

Description: Right-eyed. Eyed side usually uniform brown to olive brown but may have white speckles. Dorsal and ventral fin edges dark. Blind side white to pale yellow tinged with reddish brown. Body elongate, diamond shaped. Small head is slender and pointed. Caudal fin nearly square with slight point at center. Lateral line nearly straight with slight curve; long accessory dorsal branch. Mouth small and asymmetric. Jaws stronger on blind side. Maxillary extends to anterior edge of lower eye. High, narrow ridge between eyes. Anal spine strong. Scales smooth at anterior part of body and rough at posterior.

Size: To 61 cm (24 inches). Average size in commercial catch (mostly females) is about 14 inches and ¾ pound.

Range and Habitat: Bering Sea and Aleutian Islands to San Cristobal Bay, Baja California. On sand bottom from 0 to 300 fm. Young are intertidal. Commercial quantities caught at 15 to 80 fm.

Remarks: Important commercial species caught by trawl. Good flavor. May have iodine flavor that is acceptable and even desirable in some markets.

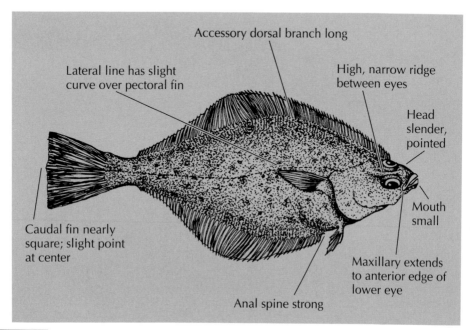

Accessory dorsal branch long

Lateral line has slight curve over pectoral fin

High, narrow ridge between eyes

Head slender, pointed

Mouth small

Caudal fin nearly square; slight point at center

Maxillary extends to anterior edge of lower eye

Anal spine strong

English sole, eyed side.

English sole, blind side.

(C-O turbot, mottled turbot, popeye sole, spot flounder)

Description: Right-eyed. Eyed side dark brown to black with lighter mottling, usually with dark spot at middle of body. Dark crescent surrounding dark circle on tail looks like inverted C-O. Blind side creamy white, sometimes with dark blotches. All fins very dark. Body deep oval shape. Caudal peduncle wide. Caudal fin rounded. Lateral line almost straight. Long accessory dorsal branch reaches to midpoint of body. Mouth small. Maxillary reaches anterior to lower eye. Eyes large, protruding, closely set. Prominent ridge between eyes. Anal spine small. First 5 to 6 dorsal fin rays insert on blind side with origin of fin level with upper lip.

Size: To 36 cm (14 inches).

Range and Habitat: Sitka, Alaska, to San Quintin Bay, Baja California. On both soft and hard bottoms from 0 to 191 fm. Usually in water less than 10 fm.

Remarks: Edibility good. Filleting is difficult because of small size and tough skin. Similar to hornyhead turbot, which has spine at front of bony ridge between eyes; and spotted turbot, which has a different pattern of dark markings on body. Can be confused with curlfin sole, which has the first 9 to 12 dorsal fin rays on the blind side.

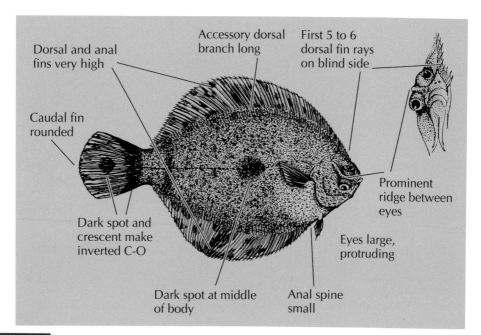

Dorsal and anal fins very high

Accessory dorsal branch long

First 5 to 6 dorsal fin rays on blind side

Caudal fin rounded

Dark spot and crescent make inverted C-O

Dark spot at middle of body

Anal spine small

Prominent ridge between eyes

Eyes large, protruding

C-O sole, eyed side.

C-O sole, blind side.

Curlfin Sole *Pleuronichthys decurrens*

(California turbot, curlfin turbot)

Description: Right-eyed. Eyed side yellowish or reddish brown to dark brown or black, usually with brown or grey mottling. Fins dark; dorsal and anal fins high. Blind side white. Body deep oval shape. Caudal fin rounded. Lateral line has slight curve over pectoral fin; long accessory dorsal branch reaches to midpoint of body. Mouth small. Maxillary extends to below anterior part of lower eye. Eyes large, closely set. High, bony ridge between eyes with tubercle or blunt spine at each end. Has 2 or 3 bony tubercles on head behind upper eye. Anal spine present. First 9 to 12 dorsal fin rays are on blind side. Origin of dorsal fin level with lower corner of mouth.

Size: To 37 cm (15 inches).

Range and Habitat: Bering Sea to San Quintin Bay, Baja California. On soft bottoms from 4 to 291 fm. Most found above 50 fm.

Remarks: Edibility very good. Moderately important in California trawl fishery. Similar to spotted and hornyhead turbots, which have 4 to 6 dorsal fin rays inserted on blind side.

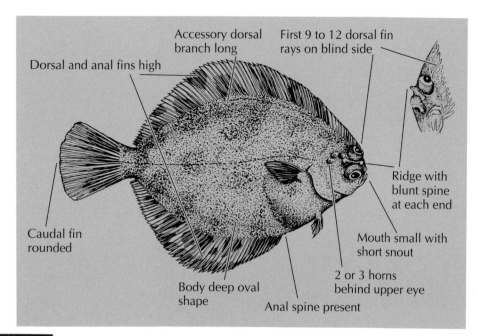

Accessory dorsal branch long

First 9 to 12 dorsal fin rays on blind side

Dorsal and anal fins high

Ridge with blunt spine at each end

Caudal fin rounded

Mouth small with short snout

Body deep oval shape

2 or 3 horns behind upper eye

Anal spine present

Curlfin sole, eyed side.

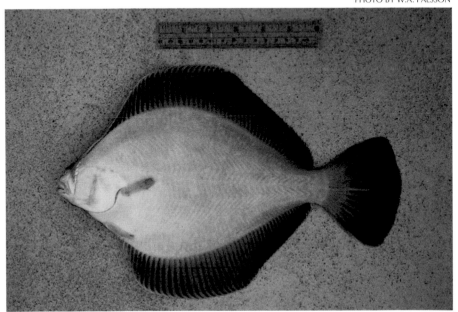

Curlfin sole, blind side.

Spotted Turbot
Pleuronichthys ritteri

(Catalina sanddab)

Description: Right-eyed. Eyed side brown to gray with light speckling, with two distinct dark spots along lateral line and two more at ends of dorsal and anal fins. Blind side white. Body shape oval. Caudal fin rounded. Lateral line almost straight; accessory dorsal branch long. Low, flat ridge between eyes. Anal spine present. First 5 or 6 rays of dorsal fin on blind side with first ray above level of mouth.

Size: To 29 cm (11 inches).

Range and Habitat: Morro Bay, central California, to Magdalena Bay, southern Baja California. From 1 to 25 fm. Found in bays and lagoons as well as offshore.

Remarks: Common inshore. Similar to hornyhead turbot, which has sharp spine at rear of ridge between eyes; and to curlfin sole, which has 9 to 12 dorsal fin rays inserted on blind side.

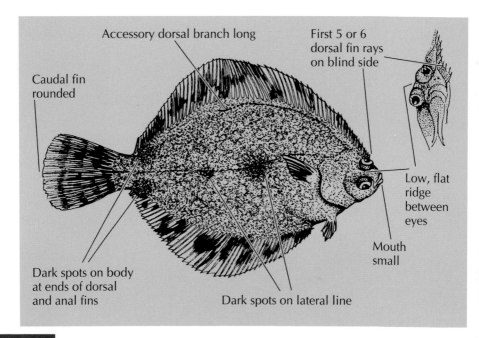

Accessory dorsal branch long

First 5 or 6 dorsal fin rays on blind side

Caudal fin rounded

Low, flat ridge between eyes

Mouth small

Dark spots on body at ends of dorsal and anal fins

Dark spots on lateral line

Spotted turbot, eyed side.

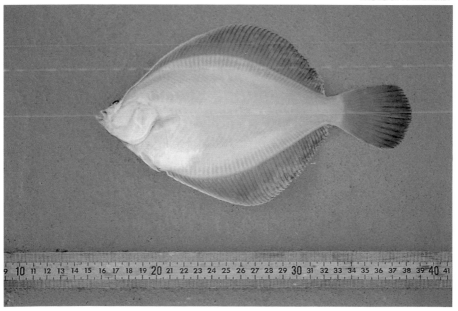

Spotted turbot, blind side.

Hornyhead Turbot
Pleuronichthys verticalis

(sharpridge flounder)

Description: Right-eyed. Eyed side yellowish brown to dark brown with gray mottling, sometimes with pale blotches. Blind side white. Body shape oval. Lateral line almost straight; accessory dorsal branch long. Mouth small with teeth only on blind side. Maxillary reaches below anterior part of lower eye. High, narrow, bony ridge between eyes with sharp spine pointing posterior at rear end. Blunt spine anterior to lower eye overhangs mouth. Anal spine present. First 4 to 6 dorsal fin rays insert on blind side.

Size: To 37 cm (15 inches). Usual size about 6 inches and a little less than 1 pound.

Range and Habitat: Oregon to Magdalena Bay, southern Baja California, and in Gulf of California. Common along southern California coast. Found in bays and sloughs. On soft bottom from 5 to 110 fm.

Remarks: Edibility fair. Similar to spotted turbot and C-O sole, both of which have teeth in lower jaw on eyed side. Also similar to curlfin sole, which has 9 to 12 dorsal fin rays on blind side.

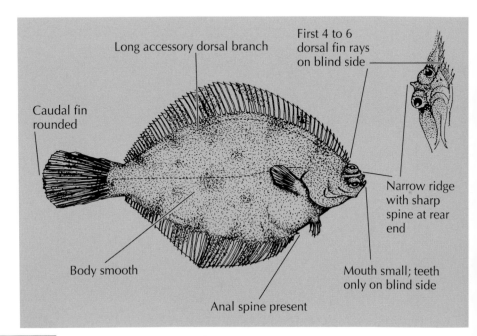

Long accessory dorsal branch

First 4 to 6 dorsal fin rays on blind side

Caudal fin rounded

Narrow ridge with sharp spine at rear end

Body smooth

Mouth small; teeth only on blind side

Anal spine present

Hornyhead turbot, eyed side.

Hornyhead turbot, blind side.

Sand Sole — *Psettichthys melanostictus*

(fringe sole, sand flounder, spotted flounder)

Description: Right-eyed. Eyed side light green or gray to brown with fine, dark brown to black speckles. Skin on eyed side has the feel of fine sandpaper. Dorsal and anal fins often have dull yellow on edges. Blind side white. Body shape elongate to oval. Caudal fin rounded. Lateral line has slight curve over pectoral fin; accessory dorsal branch short to moderate. Mouth large with large teeth. Maxillary extends below middle of lower eye. Eyes small with flat, wide space between them. Anal spine strong. First few dorsal fin rays elongate and mostly free of membrane.

Size: To 63 cm (25 inches) and over 5 pounds.

Range and Habitat: Bering Sea and Aleutian Islands to Redondo Beach, southern California. From near shore to 178 fm. A shallow water species usually found above 40 fm. Prefers sandy bottom.

Remarks: Fine food fish. Common and often caught by sport fishermen from shore. A minor part of the commercial trawl catch.

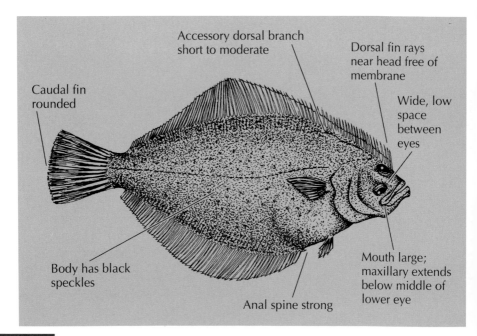

Accessory dorsal branch short to moderate

Dorsal fin rays near head free of membrane

Caudal fin rounded

Wide, low space between eyes

Body has black speckles

Mouth large; maxillary extends below middle of lower eye

Anal spine strong

Family: Pleuronectidae

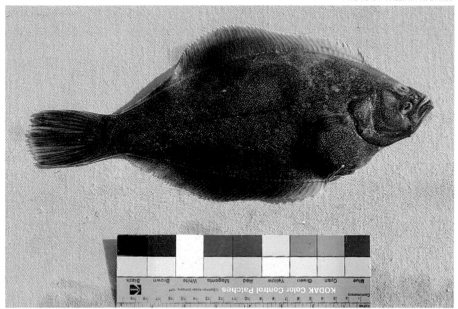

Sand sole, eyed side.

Sand sole, blind side.

Greenland Halibut *Reinhardtius hippoglossoides*

(Greenland turbot, lesser halibut, Newfoundland turbot)

Description: Right-eyed. Eyed side very dark brown to purplish black. Blind side dark gray, usually with lighter speckling. Fish is elongate, diamond-shaped. Caudal fin slightly concave. Lateral line almost straight with slight slope over pectoral fin; accessory dorsal branch absent. Mouth very large with strong conical teeth. Maxillary extends below posterior part of lower eye or beyond. Eyes small with flat, wide space between them. Upper eye on dorsal ridge is visible from blind side. L-shaped (angular) preopercle has 4 or 5 large pores along lower and posterior margins. Anal spine absent.

Size: To 120 cm (47 inches) and over 25 pounds. Average size in trawl catches is about 25 inches and 5 to 9 pounds.

Range and Habitat: In arctic waters and northern Atlantic and Pacific Oceans. In Sea of Japan and Sea of Okhotsk. From Chukchi Sea south to Coronado Islands, northern Baja California. Rare south of Alaska. Taken from 7 to 1,094 fm. Primarily a deepwater species.

Remarks: A good food fish and commercially important. Similar to arrowtooth and Kamchatka flounders, which have crescent-shaped preopercle and lighter blind side.

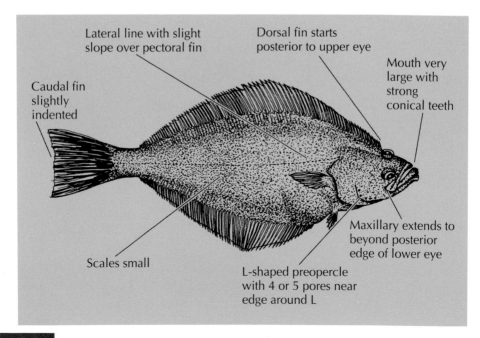

Lateral line with slight slope over pectoral fin

Dorsal fin starts posterior to upper eye

Mouth very large with strong conical teeth

Caudal fin slightly indented

Scales small

L-shaped preopercle with 4 or 5 pores near edge around L

Maxillary extends to beyond posterior edge of lower eye

Greenland halibut, eyed side.

Greenland halibut, blind side.

Glossary

The following terms for describing flatfish are defined as used in this guide-book and in the references listed in it.

Abdominal ridge: The margin along the ventral edge of a flatfish separating the eyed and blind sides.

Accessory dorsal branch (ADB): A branch of the lateral line running from near the head and back toward the tail, just below the base of the dorsal fin.

Anal fin: An unpaired fin on the ventral side of the body between the anus and the tail.

Anal spine: A hard, sharp spine pointing anterior and located anterior to the anal fin.

Anterior: Of, related to, or toward the front or head end.

Anus: The posterior external opening of the digestive tract; the vent.

Asymmetrical: Not symmetrical; one side is not a mirror image of the other.

Blind side: The bottom side of a flatfish. This side lacks eyes and usually has little or no pigmentation.

Caudal fin: The tail fin.

Caudal peduncle: The narrow fleshy end of the body that supports the caudal fin.

Confluent: A term used to describe adjoining fins that run into each other with little or no break between them.

Deciduous: Describes scales that are easily detached.

Dextral: Right-eyed; has both eyes on right side and lies on left side, as opposed to sinistral.

Dorsal fin: An unpaired fin on the dorsal or upper side of the body, between the head and the tail.

Dorsal ridge: The margin along the dorsal edge of a flatfish separating the eyed and blind sides.

Dorsal spine: Hard, usually sharp fin supports found in anterior part of dorsal fin in some fishes.

Double truncate: Refers to the caudal fin shape that is indented above and below the center; longer parts are at edges and at center.

Elongate: Body shape stretched out; notably long in relation to width.

Eyed side: The top side of a flatfish. This side has eyes and is more darkly pigmented than the side that lies against the bottom.

Fork length: The measurement from the farthest anterior projection of the head to the tips of the middle rays of the caudal fin.

Gill arch: The foundation or bony support of the gill.

Gill cavity: Chamber at the back and bottom of the head that contains the gills.

Gill cover: The bony covering of the gill cavity composed of the opercular bones; the operculum.

Gill filament: Long projections from the posterior side of the gill arches that extract oxygen from the water.

Gill raker: A bony, toothlike structure on the anterior edge of the gill arch used for protection or for straining out food.

Head length: The measurement from the tip of the snout (upper jaw) to the farthest edge of the gill cover.

Indented: Refers to the crescent-shaped caudal fin.

Interorbital space: The space on top of the head between the bony edges of the orbits or eye sockets.

Lateral line: A series of modified scales with pore-like openings to a sensory canal along the side of a fish.

Lunate: Refers to the caudal fin shape that is indented and looks like a crescent.

Mandible: The lower jaw.

Maxillaries: A pair of bones that form the back part of the upper jaw and often have teeth.

Median fin: An unpaired fin lying on the midline that divides the fish into right and left halves, such as dorsal and anal fins.

Ocellus: A round to oval eyelike pigment spot (plural is ocelli).

Opercle: The large, rectangular bone that forms most of the gill cover.

Operculum: The bony covering of the gill cavity composed of the opercular bones; the gill cover.

Paired fins: Pectoral and pelvic fins that occur in pairs, in contrast to unpaired median fins.

Pectoral fins: The uppermost of two sets of paired fins.

Pelvic fins: Paired fins on ventral part of body; also called ventral fins. They may be near anus, below pectoral fins, or near throat.

Peritoneum: The inner lining of the abdominal cavity.

Pointed: Refers to the caudal fin shape that is pointed at the center.

Pore: A sensory organ in the skin of fish consisting of a blind opening or pit.

Posterior: Of, related to, or toward the rear or tail end.

Premaxillaries: A pair of bones that form the front part of the upper jaw and usually have teeth.

Preopercle: The most anterior bone in the gill cover, lying anterior to the opercle.

Protuberance: An outward bulge.

Ray: A flexible, jointed rod that supports the fin membrane.

Rounded: Refers to the caudal fin shape that curves in a convex arc.

Sinistral: Left-eyed; has both eyes on left side and lies on right side, as opposed to dextral.

Snout length: The measurement from the tip of the snout (upper jaw) to the anterior edge of the orbit.

Spine: A fin support that is more or less stiffened and may have a sharp tip. Spines do not branch and do not have obvious segments.

Square: Refers to shape of caudal fin that is nearly straight, as though cut off.

Standard length: The measurement from the farthest anterior projection of the head to the base of the caudal fin (where it joins the body).

Stellate: Starlike in shape or arrangement.

Strong (anal spine): Well developed, easy to find (see weak anal spine).

Subopercle: The bone in the gill cover below the opercle.

Symmetrical: Having one side the mirror image of the other.

Truncate: Refers to the caudal fin shape that is nearly straight, as though cut off.

Tubercle: A lump or projection on the surface, usually a modified scale.

Tuberculate: Covered with tubercles.

Unpaired fins: Median fins.

Vent: The posterior external opening of the digestive tract; the anus.

Ventral fins: Paired fins on the lower part of the body; may be near anus, below pectoral fins, or near throat; also called pelvic fins.

Vomer: A bone, usually bearing teeth, at the front part of the roof of the mouth.

Weak (anal spine): Small, difficult to find (see strong anal spine).

Selected References

Following are some of the references and guidebooks used in preparing this publication. They will provide additional information on the species covered in the guide. Many scientific papers that were consulted in the preparation of this field guide are not included here.

Allen, M.J., and G.B. Smith. 1988. Atlas and zoogeography of common fishes in the Bering Sea and Northeastern Pacific. NOAA Technical Report NMFS 66:115-133.

Baxter, R. 1990. Annotated key to the fishes of Alaska. Red Mountain (Homer), Alaska: Arctic-Bio, 803 pp.

Bykov, V.P. 1985. Marine fishes: Chemical composition and processing properties. Rotterdam, The Netherlands: A.A. Balkema.

Eschmeyer, W.N., E.S. Herald, H. Hamann, and K.P. Smith. 1984. A field guide to Pacific Coast fishes of North America from the Gulf of Alaska to Baja California. Boston: Houghton-Mifflin, 336 pp.

Gotshall, D.W. 1981. Pacific Coast inshore fishes. Los Osos, California: Sea Challengers.

Hart, J.L. 1973. Pacific fishes of Canada. Fish. Res. Board of Can. Bull. 180, 740 pp.

International Pacific Halibut Commission. 1987. The Pacific halibut: Biology, fishery, and management. IPHC Technical Report 22 (Revision of 6 and 16), 59 pp.

Kessler, D.W. 1985. Alaska's saltwater fishes and other sea life. Anchorage: Alaska Northwest Publ. Co., 359 pp.

Lamb, A., and P. Edgell. 1986. Coastal fishes of the Pacific Northwest. Madeira Park, B.C., Canada: Harbour Publ. Co., 224 pp.

Lee, R.S. 1979. White fish identification guide. Fairbanks: Univ. of Alaska Sea Grant College Program. MAB No. 9, 169 pp.

Miller, D.J., D. Gotshall, and R. Nitsos. 1965. A field guide to some common ocean sport fishes of California. Sacramento: California Dept. of Fish and Game, 87 pp.

Miller, D.J., and R.N. Lea. 1972. Guide to coastal marine fishes of California. Sacramento: California Dept. of Fish and Game. Fish. Bull. 157, 235 pp.

Orr, J., D. Baker, and M. Brown. 1992. Field key to the flatfishes from Point Conception to the Arctic. (Draft.) 11 pp.

Pereyra, W.T., J.E. Reeves, and R.G. Bakkala. 1976. Demersal and shellfish resources of the eastern Bering Sea in the baseline year 1975. NOAA Processed Report NMFS, 619 pp.

Quast, J.C., and E. Hall. 1972. List of fishes of Alaska and adjacent waters with a guide to some of their literature. Washington, D.C.: National Marine Fisheries Service. Technical Report NMFS SSRF-658, 47 pp.

Robins, C.R., R.M. Bailey, C.E. Bond, J.R. Brooker, E.A. Lachner, R.N. Lea, and W.B. Scott. 1991. Common and scientific names of fishes from the United States and Canada. American Fisheries Society Special Publication 20 (Fifth Edition), 183 pp.

Sakamoto, K. 1984. Interrelationships of the family Pleuronectidae (Pisces: Pleuronectiformes). Mem. Fac. Fish. Hokkaido Univ. 31(1-2):95-215.

Somerton, D., and C. Murray. 1976. Field guide to the fish of Puget Sound and the Northwest Coast. Seattle: Univ. of Washington Press, 70 pp.

Wilimovsky, N.J. 1954. List of the fishes of Alaska. Stanford Ichthyol. Bull. 4(5):279-294.

Wilimovsky, N.J. 1958. Provisional keys to the fishes of Alaska. Juneau: U.S. Fish and Wildlife Service, Fish. Res. Laboratory, 113 pp.

Index

Note: **Bolded** text indicates common and scientific names recommended by the American Fisheries Society (AFS). For species not on the AFS list of North American species, **bolded** text indicates currently accepted common and scientific names.